Wataru & Yuichi

The Left Hand Dreams of Him

ONLY THE RING FINGER KNOWS

VOLUME 2
THE LEFT HAND DREAMS OF HIM

Written by
SATORU KANNAGI

Illustrations by
HOTARU ODAGIRI

English translation by
Duane Johnson

June

Los Angeles

ONLY THE RING FINGER KNOWS VOL. 2
THE LEFT HAND DREAMS OF HIM

Written by Satoru Kannagi
Illustrated by Hotaru Odagiri
English translation by Duane Johnson

English Edition Published by
DIGITAL MANGA PUBLISHING
A division of DIGITAL MANGA, Inc.
1487 W 178th Street, Suite 300
Gardena, CA 90248

www.dmpbooks.com

Library of Congress Cataloging-in-Publication Data - Available Upon Request

First Edition: April 2006
ISBN: 1-56970-885-1
10 9 8 7 6 5 4 3 2 1

Printed in China

ONLY THE RING FINGER KNOWS

Other ONLY THE RING FINGER KNOWS books
published by Digital Manga Publishing

Contents

The Left Hand Dreams of Him

T he gentle morning light filled his half-opened eyes.
Blinking several times, Wataru Fujii quietly looked over beside him.

...No way. He's still asleep...

Immediately next to him, breathing peacefully and dreaming, was his boyfriend Yuichi Kazuki. Considering how often Yuichi had smiled half-ruefully as he woke Wataru up just in time not to be late, what in the world was going on this morning?

Wow...his face is pretty cute when he's sleeping...

Feeling that he'd made some kind of gain, Wataru cheerfully peered at Yuichi's relaxed face.

Compared to Wataru, with his spirited honest eyes and slightly saucy expression, the ever-graceful smile and mature composure of Yuichi, who was a year older, was unforgettable. For this reason, when they walked beside each other they'd sometimes been told reluctantly by friends that they looked like a mischievous younger brother and an honor student older brother.

"It can't be helped, though. Kazuki's too good to be true..."

Wataru pouted his lips and spoke a little bitterly.

This past spring, Yuichi's good grades had easily gotten him into a national university that was rumored to be tough to enter. He was currently enrolled in the general education science department, and he took advantage of this and rented an apartment near the college. The two lovers had thus been able to spend sweet nights together without anyone watching over them. Even if it didn't happen every week, Wataru's pajamas, tooth brush, and a change of clothes were there, as if they were expected to be.

So, there had been chances to stare at his sleeping face like this before.

"Even so...what a pretty smile he has..."

Looking at the graceful curves of his profile, an unconscious sigh spilled from Wataru. He could never tell Yuichi a line like that while he was awake, though -- he'd be made fun of for showing such weakness. He could easily hear him saying "Well, that's stupid!" in a mocking voice, ten-odd centimeters away from him, peering at him with a slightly malicious look in his eyes.

But the only time it was different was when he was asleep. While still in bed, Wataru put his chin in his hands with an air of satisfaction, and casually shifted his gaze to the ring on his own left ring finger.

When rings were in-vogue at their high school, Yuichi, who was either popular with or admired by the entire student body, and Wataru, a very ordinary student, accidentally got their rings of the same design mixed-up.

In the end, it was revealed that Yuichi had had feelings for Wataru and secretly had his own ring made to match his. After many twists and turns, the two of them had reached their own happy ending.

After everything, they still each had the silver rings shining on their fingers.

Of course, neither of them took theirs off carelessly. In fact, while they were loving each other the night before, by some chance Wataru had heard the clinking sound of the two rings hitting each other. It had been such a sweet moment, the two of them had unthinkingly burst out laughing.

"Hn... "

Maybe because Wataru looked too intently and for too long, faint wrinkles began to show on Yuichi's forehead. Uh oh, thought Wataru as he averted his eyes, and presently Yuichi's eyes opened slowly.

"...Wataru...what're you doing?"

"Huh? Uh, nothing..."

"You do some creepy things! How long have you been watching me sleep?"

As-feared, Yuichi seemed resolved to be unhappy. Waking up with strange quickness, he sat up and blew out a breath that pushed his hair up.

"I was careless. I never thought you'd wake up before me. It's only 7:00."

"S-Sorry for waking up early!

"That's right, apologize. You really are rude."

"Do you have to go that far...?"

In any case, it seemed that Yuichi was quite reluctant to let Wataru see his sleeping face. After throwing a quick icy glance his way, he looked at Wataru's sullen expression and raised the edges of his lips sarcastically.

"Well, maybe you finally have that much time on your hands now. Wataru, you're somewhat used to this by now, right?"

"Eh... Used to what...?

It's almost been two months since I started living on my own. In that time you've come to stay over almost every week.

"Y-Yeah..."

"Thanks to that, we're both likely to lose sleep. But there's no helping that, is there?"

"Kazuki..."

Wataru guessed what Yuichi was getting at, and his face suddenly turned red. As if seeing this finally put him in a better mood, this time Yuichi smiled fully and poked Wataru's cheek with his index finger.

"Have you got some objection?"

"Well, at first I definitely...you know, there were so many thing I didn't know about... But, lately, well..."

"And now that we aren't disturbed, we can lose ourselves more in things. Maybe it's thanks to that, but I'm happy that you've become more active too, Wataru."

"A-Active...?"

"It's been almost a year since we got together. Don't you wonder if we've become used to each other? You know, in different ways?"

"...Stop talking dirty, you pervert."

As Wataru rubbed the spot that had been poked and looked up reproachfully, Yuichi smiled and brought their faces close together. Who does creepy things? went through Wataru's head automatically. He actually looks happy to see me angry and confused. The proof of that is how he could poke me in the cheek and then unabashedly move his lip to say:

"I love you, Wataru."

"......"

"You love me too, don't you?"

He could move his lips a little like that, as if he doesn't care at all about it. He could keep giving Wataru light kisses until all resolve and strength had drained from him.

"Strictly speaking, it's the first time I've ever slept with anyone either."

The first time they had been together, Yuichi revealed that in a whisper and surprised Wataru. That's how mature Yuichi seemed in bed. His actions, full of loving care and consideration, enveloped Wataru's heart when he felt he was about to be crushed by nerves.

Purely out of curiosity, Wataru tried asking a question. "How about not strictly speaking?"…but even now, he hadn't heard the answer. What was certain was that Yuichi's kindness hadn't changed from the start. His fingers would touch him with delicate grace, and he would be affectionate towards each one of Wataru's responses. If that was what he meant, Wataru seriously didn't think the day would ever come when he got used to being in his arms.

"I love you...Kazuki..."

He whispered in a voice on the verge of vanishing as he supported Yuichi's weight with his whole body. Unaware of the soft smile that graced his boyfriend's face as he heard the words, Wataru was then and there swept away by a renewed passion.

"...Geez, this is borin'."

Tossing the mechanical pencil in his hand, Kawamura let loose a dejected sigh above his notebook. Wataru, who'd been solving a math formula in the opposite seat, stared fixedly with upturned eyes at his buddy's face.

"Ah...what? What's that cold look for?"

"Kawamura, look. Don't say things that'll make your bad attitude contagious."

"Saying that won't make it any less boring. What can you do?"

Then I wish you wouldn't say "Let's do homework together in the library after school." As he glared at him with that criticism in-mind too, Kawamura's face suddenly distorted miserably.

"Tch, must be nice to be you. You've got an exclusive tutor who ranked 27th in the nationwide model exam."

"Exclusive...hey!"

"Well, on last week's midterm, didn't you climb up to around #30? I was a rank C for my first-choice college."

"I was outside the ranking range."

Wataru answered in the blink of an eye, and for a moment Kawamura was speechless. Then he asked "Eh..." in return.

"Please, Wataru. Spare me the bad..."

"But it's true. I tried picking the same college as Kazuki, and I was outside the range. Laughable, huh?"

"Well...it's a reckless thing to do."

In an obviously let-down fashion, Kawamura

leaned back against his chair.

The "nationwide model exam 27th place" he just mentioned was, of course, Yuichi. If a college on the level of someone like his was easy to get into, no one would have any problems.

"Well, so what, I mean why force yourself to aim for the same college as Kazuki? Didn't you spend the whole weekend at his place again? Good for you guys."

"Huh?"

"Your cell went straight to voice mail."

"Oh, sorry..."

Wataru discreetly avoided his steady gaze out of embarrassment. Since Yuichi graduated, their chances to see each other had drastically decreased. For that reason, Yuichi turned off his cell as much as possible when they were alone. Wataru happened to fall into the same habit.

"That's because I didn't see him for so long with exams going on..."

"I don't really mind. I was going to ask what you were doing about prep school over the summer."

"Oh, right... It's that time already..."

"The popular courses hit capacity before you know it. Wataru, you want to do a private science program?"

"Yeah..."

That's right, thought Wataru as he became gloomy. Last year Yuichi had exams, so they weren't able to enjoy their new relationship as much as they'd wanted to. But, this year he was the exam student.

Right now he had time for these casual stay-over dates, but eventually their time together would lessen and he'd have to devote himself to studying.

"Just when I thought things had finally calmed down..."

I really hate being a student.

At some point, the troublesome math formula totally left Wataru's head, and he heaved an extra-large sigh that amazed even Kawamura.

The frosted glasses were set down softly before their eyes -- it was the first iced coffees they'd ordered this year. The old guy who brought them smiled courteously at the pair who hadn't been there in a while.

"Here you go. That was one without sweetener, right? It sure is nice to see you two together here."

"Well, thank you. You seem to be doing fine as usual, sir."

Yuichi bowed his head lightly and answered with his honor student-ish smile. Wataru felt chilled inside every time someone else commented on how "good" they looked together, but Yuichi didn't show signs of being perturbed at all.

"Being here with you makes it feel like I'm back in high school."

"Yeah. We were here all the time."

"As always, not a single young customer is here. That makes me feel more secure."

Yuichi was completely serious as he looked all around the small store interior nostalgically. It was a small cafe which didn't even look like one from the outside, boasting the warmth of aged wood and a peaceful atmosphere like time had stopped. It was a place that students from their school took no notice of, but it was packed with memories for Wataru and Yuichi.

"Since I graduated, it's only been you. Of students from school who come here, that is."

"...Coming here along would be boring..."

After leaving the library and Kawamura, Wataru ran over here still wearing his uniform, but the second he thought that Yuichi would never again be there waiting for him in the same uniform, he felt just a little lonely.

"Wataru, what's wrong?"

"Uh...what...?"

"Your face looks vacant. Where's the you who was whooping it up yesterday that exams are finally over?"

"W-Who was whooping anything up?"

"You were the one who woke up early and stared love-struck at my sleeping face!"

"......"

You sure are stubborn, Wataru was about to answer with, but then he closed his mouth, taken aback.

Maybe Yuichi was unexpectedly happy. From the point of view of a cool personality, having your defenseless face seen might be a disgrace, but "Wataru was enraptured with me" wasn't all there was to it, either.

The truth was, he wasn't really straightforward.

Back on campus he was indeed the honor

student, good at everything he did. Both then and now there was no end of people who adored him. Wataru smiled wryly as he reflected that he was the only one Yuichi would show his immature side to.

"...Actually, I wouldn't go so far as to say 'vacant.' I was talking with Kawamura about prep school, and it made me kind of gloomy. Now that you're finally a college student, I thought we could spend as much time together as we wanted...but now I'm the one with entrance exams."

"Haven't I been saying that since last year? Why's it just hitting you now?"

"Well, we've finally been together a year. Isn't the first year of a relationship usually the most exciting? But now I've got to get ready for exams soon, and even if I do well and place into a good school, we'll still be at different ones..."

"This is rare."

"Eh?"

"You're thinking negatively. Here I thought you were tough like a weed."

"...Now, look... "

Even though he knew he was being teased, he couldn't keep from complaining. But Yuichi's eyes softened and he shrugged his shoulders, as if to say it was all a joke.

"Seriously, your exams are something I need to think about, too. If by some chance you failed because of your relationship with me, I'd have to apologize to your parents."

"Thanks for your fine opinion!"

Wataru's lips pouted in displeasure. What he wanted to hear from Yuichi wasn't such formalities, but his honest feelings.

"You don't need to look that way, Wataru, there's nothing for you to worry about. I'll work with your schedule."

"Huh..."

Doubting his ears at the unexpected words, Wataru hurriedly shifted his gaze upwards. Yuichi had the cup level with his eyes, making the cool ice cubes clink together lightly. The straw spun around in the half-gone iced coffee, and it eased the heavy atmosphere a bit.

"Thankfully, I now have more spare time than a high school student. You can call me anytime you want to see me, even the middle of the night or at dawn. I don't mind if it's just for five minutes, or even one."

"Uh...but, that's..."

"It's better than not seeing you at all."

"Kazuki…"

If Yuichi had been planning to say this, he'd be a fairly smug guy. But, Yuichi was not a man of strategy when it came to love. Knowing that, they were the happiest words Wataru could have heard.

"Listen, Wataru."

Yuichi quietly returned the glass and put his fingers together on top of the table. The silver-colored ring on his ring finger glittered, and Wataru felt relieved for no reason.

"Let's make a deal. Neither of us will fake our way through this. Even if it means we get into a fight, honesty is by far the best policy."

"...Yeah. I hear you."

When Wataru nodded gently, a new customer entered the cafe. Yuichi froze the hand he was about to touch Wataru with, and reluctantly pulled his fingers back. But, after he let his resentment-filled gaze shift to the doorway, his eyes widened in surprise.

"Kazuki...what is it...?"

"...Nothing. Someone I know came in."

"You mean that guy?"

"Yeah. He's an upperclassman at my college."

Maybe it was imagination, but Yuichi seemed to be a bit unsettled. His facial expression didn't shift enough to indicate this, but Wataru was sensitive enough to catch it.

Wow...even rare things still happen sometimes.

Tempted by curiosity, Wataru followed the young man heading for the counter covertly with his eyes. He hadn't seemed to notice that Yuichi was there, but his focused way of walking showed that he was not a first-time customer.

Then maybe he's a new regular…

The young man exchanged friendly greetings with the old guy washing dishes, and sat down nimbly at the small counter. These casual movements were so casual and precise they were fascinating. His long legs were wrapped in faded jeans, and his pointed ankles peeked out from the cuffs. The way he wore leather sandals on his bare feet seemed at a glance simple, but judging by the polished design they had to be some brand name.

He seems really out of place somehow...

That was Wataru's honest impression.

The lighting in the cafe was fluorescent and dim, so even in daytime there was a darker tone inside than outside. It felt like the sun had suddenly trespassed its way in. But, what definitely didn't leave a bad impression was how the air around the guy seemed light and in no danger of destroying the atmosphere.

"So, he's an upperclassman..."

Wataru murmured unconsciously.

"This seems weird somehow."

"Seems weird?"

"...The you I know was already a senior. So, everyone always made so much noise about you being an upperclassman. To hear that word from your mouth seems kind of...strange."

"Dummy."

With a laugh Yuichi warded off Wataru's fainthearted impression. Then he folded his arms haughtily, and said "Sorry, but I'm a prominent freshman now." in a very un-freshman-like impudent tone.

"I see your point, though. Right now I have no interest in any cliques or clubs. The enticement to join one is of course nothing like it was in high school."

"As always, you don't like following the crowd."

"Well, even if you call him my upperclassman, it's only in that we share an elective. But then, even if he dropped the course, the professor would still praise him in rather nice Queen's English. Even I was surprised at that."

"Queen's...?"

"The elective's a speaking class."

"......"

Yuichi's casual explanation left Wataru with a suddenly sullen face. Being able to read his expression, Yuichi leaned gently towards him in a triumphant manner.

"That's because you're bad at English. But wasn't the last exam a piece of cake because I showed you what to study? You should be thankful."

"Unh...well..."

Yuichi's guidance had definitely been perfect. Thanks to the help, Wataru's rank had rapidly climbed, and even his mother, who until now frowned on his overnight stays, readily believed his excuse that he was being tutored by a former graduate.

Even given how much he had swaggered afterwards, Yuichi was indeed an excellent teacher.

"Don't worry. I'll be sure to help you with entrance exams, too. But in exchange, I'll be even stricter than your instructors. Be ready for it."

"...For-real?"

"Well, let's get going."

Laughing at the now truly pale Wataru, Yuichi stood up with the check in-hand. Perhaps not intending to say hello to the young man from the start, he turned and walked towards the register at the entrance.

"The drink was good today."

"My, my, it's been a while. Maybe the first time since you graduated?"

"Yes. I'll still drop by occasionally."

The old man who handled the money was in a good humor since his favorite, Yuichi, had come back. With a forced smile on his face, Wataru waited a bit to the side while Yuichi took care of paying.

Since arguing at the register every time was unsightly, they had recently adopted the system where Yuichi would pay for everything up-front, and then Wataru would give him his share of the bill. Wataru had kept saying that he felt uncomfortable always being treated by another man, so this was the rule they finally established.

Even so...he really is popular with people, regardless of age or gender.

With nothing else to do, Wataru watched the two of them genially exchange small talk. But he suddenly felt somebody's strong gaze upon him, and he slowly turned to look in that direction.

Eh...

He caught his breath in an instant.

The young man who was Yuichi's upperclassman was looking directly his way from the counter. His look was a bit intense compared to the refined arrangement of his face, but the unreserved stare mysteriously didn't feel impolite. Rather, a strange enveloping sensation wafted its way around Wataru.

Wha...What's this all about...?

For some reason, suddenly feeling unsettled, Wataru hurriedly averted his eyes from the young man. He had never had such "unreadable" eyes on him up to that point. It was as if, just from being looked at, his inner soul was being seen through.

Maybe...he just noticed that Kazuki was here...

Wataru forced himself to murmur in his head alone, controlling the pounding brought on by unease. But it was clearly him who was being watched, not Yuichi. A sense of cold vitality overflowed from within the young man. That scent, that touch seemed like they would ride right through the air on his gaze.

"Wataru...? What's wrong?"

"N-Nothing."

Yuichi's suspicious voice brought Wataru back to reality suddenly. When he had his wits about him once more and he looked again, the young man already had his back turned and was chatting with the old man behind the counter.

"What the..."

Wataru involuntarily let out a long breath, and felt his shoulders relax. It was just a few seconds, but his body had been extremely tense.

"Come on, or I'll leave you here."

"Ah, sorry, sorry."

He nodded to the old man, and with a fast pace followed Yuichi out of the cafe. As if worried about how odd Wataru was acting, Yuichi looked over his shoulder with a face like he was going to ask a question, but in the end he didn't say anything.

There's another, thought Yuichi as he drew a check with a red pen in the magazine he held.

"So, I guess it's tutoring or manual labor..."

About an hour must have passed since he set

up camp at a window table with a cup of coffee. In that time, Yuichi didn't so much as look at his now-cold coffee, as he was engrossed in calculating hourly wages. When his brother, twelve years older than him, was in college, it was a seller's market where good part-time work was quite easy to find, but that age had long ago seemingly reached the status of legend.

"Oh, well. Anyway, better do an interview..."

"What's got you looking so troubled?"

Suddenly, a shadow fell on his head. At the sound of the familiar voice, Yuichi silently shifted just his gaze upward. As he thought, the one looking down on him was Masanobu Asaka, a boy two years ahead of him at school.

Smiling affably, Masanobu said:

"You're very ill-prepared, Kazuki."

"...How is that, Asaka?"

"The way you're sitting in a cafe on campus zealously checking off things in a help-wanted mag. If the women saw you like that, I'm sure it'd kick up another fuss. If by some chance they found out where you work, some of them might scheme to get close to you. Even beyond that, among freshmen you're..."

"I'm sorry, but I don't plan on working where there are any women."

Interrupting Masanobu curtly, Yuichi closed the magazine and stood up. Glances began focusing intermittently on the table. Almost all of them belonged to female students.

Masanobu smiled and shrugged.

"...You see? Didn't I tell you?"

"I think half of it is your fault, though."

A bit annoyed, Yuichi looked back coldly at the upperclassman in his own world.

"I'll say it again, Asaka."

"Hm?"

"Just as I've turned it down countless times, I am not going to join your circle. While I'm certainly deeply interested in the recycling of stores and houses, I have no intention of pursuing building. Besides, everyone noticing your involvement with me is problematic."

"Well, both you and I stand out."

Masanobu answered with a magnanimous smile, gently bushing aside Yuichi's objection. One had to take care around him, as he had a way of easing doubt and winning the skeptical over with anything he said.

What's more, Masanobu's charm wasn't limited to that alone. He was tall, well-balanced, and deliberate in everything he did, so that even trivial actions were made to look beautiful. Maybe because of this, he was able to make the typical combinations of shirts, jeans, and cotton pants he liked to wear seem like something special that was beyond imitation.

Yuichi more or less had attributes similar to Masanobu's. If the two of them were next to each other, telling them not to stand out would be impossible.

"Excuse me, I need to be going."

"Oh, hold on a minute."

Bowing for form's sake, Yuichi tried to start walking. His right shoulder was suddenly tugged, and he became overtly rigid. He turned around and fixed Masanobu a bold stare of his amber eyes.

"Was that guy you were with the other day your little brother?"

"Eh..."

"Don't play innocent. You noticed I was there, but you left without saying anything. I've been going to that place a lot lately, but I never thought I'd see you there."

That's my line thought Yuichi, but wisely kept quiet. Masanobu was a sharp guy, and using his opponent's careless remarks to drag them to his own level was his specialty.

"You two sure are close."

Masanobu tossed out his remark in an untroubled voice after he took his hand away, not paying any attention to the lack of a response.

"At a glance I thought 'underclassman' or 'brother'...but maybe not given how secretive you're being."

"He goes to my high school."

Yuichi answered concisely, as there was nothing else he could do.

"The high school I went to is near that place. So sometimes I go by there."

"Ah, I see. You don't have a little brother, do you? You just have a much older, first-class architect brother."

"How did you know that...?"

It didn't show on his face, but Yuichi's heart beat harder. Masanobu had been trying to encourage him to join his circle since he first entered college, but he never thought he'd go so far as to research his family.

"He has an interesting face."

Smiling, Masanobu put his impression into words, indifferent to Yuichi's agitation.

"Interesting...you mean Wataru?"

"So, his name's Wataru. Yeah, that's right. Just looking at his face I get a clear view into his feelings. Talking to someone like that never gets boring, does it?"

"......"

"Especially for someone like you or me."

It was uncomfortable just thinking about what he could have meant. Masanobu was probably only saying what he honestly thought, but Yuichi didn't think he could calmly ignore it when the subject was Wataru.

"Afternoon lectures are starting soon, so I need to go."

Yuichi forced himself free of the subject and started walking again. He soon realized he'd left the help wanted mag behind, but he didn't feel like going back to get it.

As the season changed from spring to early summer, the color of the sky was different every day. It wasn't unusual for it to become a thicker blue day by day, only for it to suddenly cool off to a pale, chilly blue.

"According to the weather forecast, both today and tomorrow are supposed to be clear...but I doubt it."

Resting his chin in his hands on the veranda railing, Wataru narrowed his eyes and looked up at the light blue sky. Yuichi's place was a seventh floor apartment, and you could see the distant skyscrapers of the city subcenter, so the view had become a big attraction.

"You're amazing, though, Kazuki. It must have eaten up all your savings to rent this place."

"All I paid was the deposit, key money, and moving expenses. I get a remittance every month, so it's nothing amazing. Well, I do think I'd like to pay it back eventually."

Yuichi walked up next to Wataru and handed him a soda he'd gotten from the refrigerator.

"The fact that the veranda is spacious is definitely a high point for this apartment...but I never thought it'd appeal to you so much, Wataru. You stare off into the sky every time you come here."

"Hey, it's nice out here. A cool breeze blows up from below. Oh yeah, isn't your birthday coming up? Let's put some chairs and a table out here and celebrate."

"You watch too much TV."

"Well, so what? It's the first auspicious day since we got together. Last year your niece's dog ran off, the girls who crashed your party got into a brawl, and you were mad that it was a disaster. So..."

"Yeah...okay, okay..."

As if not wanting to remember it, Yuichi frowned a little and consented. They still hadn't dreamed then that a year later they'd be looking up at the sky together.

Before long, Yuichi muttered as if he was by himself:

"Instead of the veranda...why don't we escape Tokyo?"

"Huh...?"

"Like we discussed before, once summer break gets here you're going to have to focus on entrance exams.   So, why don't we go somewhere before then?   Somewhere far, somewhere close, anywhere. Somewhere you want to go..."

"Kazuki..."

Wataru looked down from the sky and stared fixedly at Kazuki's profile. He softly moved closer to his boyfriend who, perhaps embarrassed by his own proposal, refused to turn his face towards him.

"That makes me really happy...but are you sure?"

"About what?"

"I know you're looking for part-time work. At first I wondered if it was for living expenses...but is it actually..."

His hair suddenly mussed up in mid-sentence, Wataru closed his mouth in surprise. Yuichi smiled thinly as he slowly met Wataru's eyes.

"It's all messed up. Looks pretty bad."

"Uh, no, that's not what I was getting at."

"It doesn't look like it'll be in time for my birthday, but I'm serious about planning a trip. What's your answer, Wataru?"

"Uh... "

"Your   answer.   Want   to   go   somewhere together?"

"......"

Wataru couldn't answer. It was because Yuichi had made it impossible right after asking the question. The tender kiss summoned a light intoxication, and as the wind blew against him he softly gave himself over to Yuichi.

Embraced by gentle arms, he was softly engulfed by a sweet sigh spilling over from the tip of his tongue. Every time he was kissed by Yuichi, Wataru remembered a sand bar in spring. A brightly colored quiet beach he was taken to as a child.

Lit by the calm sun, the transparent sea water sparkled here and there. When he walked timidly across it, the waves washed the warm sand out from between his toes. That ticklish happiness filled Wataru's whole body every time Yuichi kissed him. It was a joy only he could give him.

The ocean would be nice, Wataru thought with a whiff.

Not that we've made any arrangements, but how amazingly ticklish would it be to exchange kisses with Yuichi at the actual beach? Just thinking about that feeling puts a smile on my face.

"What're you smiling to yourself about?"

As usual, Yuichi followed up a kiss by joking around. Wataru tried making an unpleasant face on-purpose, and quickly started thinking If we're going on a trip, I'd better find a job, too.

"Of course that's a bad idea."

Totally blocked, Wataru stopped walking and bit

back. "Why?"

"I'm not talking about working for a long time. I'll just work long enough to earn enough money for the trip, then immediately quit and devote myself to studying."

"No. You can devote yourself before that."

Yuichi looked back and repeated himself without any change in facial expression. There didn't seem to be any room for discussion about this with him.

"In any case, I'm against you working. If you'd go that far, then forget the trip. In the first place, jobs high schoolers can get don't amount to much. You're not about to find a lucrative short-term job that easily."

"W-Well...that might be true..."

"Come on, leave the expenses to me this time. Your job is to get permission from your parents to go on the trip. Whether we stay two nights or three doesn't change much."

"But..."

"You hear me?"

Yuichi said definitively, as if to say "We're done talking about this."

It all began with a help-wanted ad.

It was Sunday afternoon, and the two of them met up to see a movie then dropped by a nearby cafe, but inside was an ad posted seeking part-timers. Seeing this, Wataru casually murmured "That might work.", but it failed to evade Yuichi's notice. Thanks to his remark, they got into an argument as soon as they walked out.

"...Kazuki, that's tyrannical."

His big dark eyes colored with reproach, and Wataru tried to resist. The people coming and going on the sidewalk would first be thrown off by the air of unrest around the two of them, and then they'd show real confusion once they got the wrong idea from Yuichi's beauty. Wataru didn't like that, either.

"You know, why do you seem to want to cop an authoritative attitude with me? We're only a year apart, and yet you're always trying to treat me to food and drinks, and you're always ordering me around. Are you that much of an adult?"

"At least more than you are."

Yuichi answered back coldly, not agitated in the least.

"Unlike you, Wataru, I don't fly off the handle all of a sudden and raise my voice on the street. Look, we're the center of attention."

"So what? That's because you're..."

"Better than average and cool, right?"

His sentence suddenly finished for him, Wataru came up short. A large palm brushed his back lightly as if to pacify him.

"Wataru's got a small frame but a big voice."

"Eh... "

Though it wasn't clear when he had approached, there was a young man standing right next to them. His white work shirt was stained here and there with soot and paint, and the knees of his worn-out jeans were completely white. Despite that, he wore the same cool expression that suited him most naturally.

"Oh, from the other day..."

"Yup. You hadn't forgotten?"

Answering Wataru's phrase in an amiable tone, he took his hand from his back and held it out anew.

"I failed to introduce myself. I'm Masanobu Asaka, a junior in the science department at the same college as Kazuki. Nice to meet you, Wataru."

"...How do you know my name...?"

"I heard it from Kazuki, of course."

The fingers awaiting Wataru's hand before him were long and finely shaped, like a musician's.

If there'd been a silver ring shining on his ring finger, he might have mistaken him for Kazuki. As Wataru thought this and began to extend his right hand, his arm was jerked roughly. Before he was even sure who had done it, he heard Yuichi's sharp voice.

"What are you doing here, Asaka?"

"What am I...what are you two doing here? You're a little old to be quarreling in the middle of the street. It would grieve your fans to see it, Kazuki."

"Please stop making fun of me. Why are you dressed like that in the first place...?"

"Ahh, this? I was just in the middle of working. See, if you go down that alley, the project we're promoting is on the right."

A small truck was just then slowly entering the alley Masanobu pointed to. Stacked in the bed was a mountain of boards of various sizes. Maybe they're building a house, thought Wataru, inclining his head. Maybe because he read his expression, Masanobu laughed lightly.

"It's my circle's activity. The Renovation

Research Society. I'm the one responsible there, and I've been trying to talk to Kazuki about it ever since he started school, but he keeps giving me the cold shoulder.

"Reno...vation...?"

Wataru became more and more confused by the unfamiliar word. He noticed that Yuichi seemed to want to leave at once, but because this was an upperclassman he couldn't cop a pushy attitude and was instead just irritated.

"Seeing is believing. If you'd like, come along with me. It won't take too long. ...Why not, Kazuki?"

"......"

Masanobu's voice kept its cheerful tone to the end, but a faint provocation could be sensed. At this unexpected development Wataru glanced at Yuichi, and it was obvious he was confused. This isn't like Yuichi at all. Maybe this is his first time having to relate to Masanobu's type and it's throwing him off.

"Okay, we'll come see it for a bit."

"Wataru..."

"It's nearby, right? So as not to get in the way of the work, we'll take a quick look and then be on our way."

For some reason Wataru was unable to keep quiet, and before he knew it he'd blurted his remark out suddenly. Yuichi looked at him in surprise, but Masanobu, on the contrary, looked at him with eyes full of satisfaction.

"I'm happy to hear you say that."

The innocent sound of his words instantly shook Wataru's emotions.

The place Masanobu stopped was a plain, isolated wooden house. It was two-storied with a blue-tiled roof. There were some cracks in the walls, and the entrance had a sliding door instead of an open-shut door.

"Built thirty-five years ago. It's my mother's home."

"So...by 'project'..."

"Asaka's circle is comprised almost completely of architectural students. Their research theme is the renovation of modern architecture...to put it simply, recycling. They remodel old buildings, and thus they're reborn for some other useful purpose."

Yuichi, who'd be silent until then, recited the summary in a flat voice. It seemed he'd been given the explanation so many times by Masanobu, he'd memorized it. Even so, Wataru still looked like he wasn't grasping it, so Masanobu took over the rest.

"Hey, Wataru."

"Yes?"

"You see old storehouses turned into restaurants, and private houses remodeled into bars in magazines a lot, right? That's basically what this is."

"But...this is an ordinary house... Aren't mansions or large buildings usually used...?"

"Like old housing restoration? Right, it's similar but a little different. It's not so grand a project as that...well, anyway, why not come in and see? That's probably the quickest way to understand."

Masanobu beckoned with his hand on the sliding door and a mischievous look on his face. Walking in nervously from behind Yuichi, Wataru couldn't believe what suddenly opened before his eyes.

"No way...it's so spacious..."

His voice unthinkingly spilled from him. The dark, confined image he had imagined by the oldness of the exterior was completely overturned.

All that was left on the first floor was the stairway, and the flat wood floor from the entryway had been renewed. Sunlight poured in like a flood from the courtyard to the wide space created by the walls of each room having been knocked down. The thick supports linking floor and ceiling were polished to a luster of amber.

"We plan to make the first floor a gallery and the second floor a small cafe with photo and art collections."

"Will it...be your cafe, Asaka...?"

"Oh, no way. I know the person who bought this place, and they're letting our circle practice on it. The work process will get coverage, so that they get publicity and an article at the same time.

"Not bad..."

Yuichi muttered these words to himself as if impressed. It was practically another world, separated by just a sliding door. The sight before him was almost beyond his imagination.

"We've already had the basic remodeling construction done by pro carpenters. All that's left for us to do is the interior design and it's done. But, while we build this everyone is jointly contributing ideas for making an atmosphere of exhibition and production, so it's rather..."

"You're so slow, Asaka. How far did you go just to buy juice?"

"Where're my smokes, man?"

"The truck is waiting in the parking area."

Before Masanobu could finish speaking, about seven or eight people stopped working and shuffled in together. The gender ratio was about even, and they looked dirty like Masanobu, but they also looked like they were kindergartners having fun in the sand.

"Oh, we have guests."

Before long, one woman's eyes fastened on Wataru and Yuichi standing behind Masanobu. Next, the face of the short woman next to her suddenly blushed.

"Wow, it's Kazuki the freshman!"

"Oh, it really is. How unusual."

"Not bad, Asaka. You finally dragged him in? Yuichi Kazuki, said to be impervious to the invitations of any and all circles? Not bad at all."

"No, he's just here to take a look. I met him on the street by coincidence. And I must confess, I forgot the juice and cigarettes. Sorry."

"What?!"

Masanobu quickly hung his head as voices of criticism erupted at him. But the air of harmony didn't change, and Wataru ended up feeling envious of this for some reason.

It was the same with Yuichi, but Wataru had no experience being a part of club activities, and even though he had friends, he had no one he could call a true "comrade." He hadn't been interested in the first place, so it wasn't as if he'd ever felt too jealous, but there must have been a unique pleasantness about being engrossed in something and working together with other people with a common goal. Their excited expressions truly suggested as much.

"By the way, who's he?"

Maybe in deference to how Yuichi seemed a bit uncomfortable about everyone fussing over him, another young man suddenly shifted the focus to Wataru.

"He's not...a college student, is he?"

"His name's Wataru Fujii. I went to his high school."

"H...Hello."

At Yuichi's cover-up line, Wataru became flustered and hung his head. But, the instant he saw his own left hand from the corner of his down-turned eyes, he erupted into a full-body cold sweat.

Oh no. The rings...we're wearing them...

Having once lost it, Wataru basically would not take his ring off...and definitely not on a day like today when he met up with Yuichi. However, it was probably inevitable that once it was known the two of them had matching rings, they'd get funny looks from everyone. Then, if strange rumors spread around campus, it would almost certainly cause problems for Yuichi.

We're in trouble. What should I do...

Now that he'd started dwelling on it, Wataru's ring finger felt heavier. He knew it'd be best to take it off at once, but he couldn't grab hold of the right timing. Now, he furiously regretted coming along in the first place.

It's all college students anyway, so this place has nothing to do with me...

Yuichi was one thing, but this was all a part of an "unreachable" college, anyway. With even that miserable thought in mind, Wataru inadvertently started becoming depressed.

"I'll go out again for juice and cigarettes. Wataru, sorry, but could you help me?"

"Eh...?"

Grasping his abruptly stiffened left hand, Masanobu peered into Wataru's eyes, looking for consent.

"Ahh! Why are you holding hands if you're just going shopping? Talk about shady!"

"Asaka likes them younger!"

"As long as they're cute, they're all fair game."

Everyone had shifted attention from the bewildered Wataru once they noticed and grew interested in the clasped hands. But maybe this kind of behavior wasn't unusual on Masanobu's part, since no one seriously seemed to think it was a problem.

Except one person.

"Uh, uh...Asaka..."

"Hey, I'll treat you to some juice."

It would be more accurate to say Wataru's left hand was engulfed rather than gently held, but it provided a good excuse for hiding the ring so he couldn't flatly shake his way free. Feeling Yuichi's gaze burning into his back, he was led outside as if dragged by Masanobu.

"A-Asaka...!"

"......"

"Asaka, um, I..."

"Yeah, I know. Sorry."

A step beyond the sliding door, the joking tone vanished from Masanobu's voice. His profile became completely serious, and he let go of the hand he'd grasped.

"You can take the ring off now."

"Uh... "

"It's all right. None of the others noticed. I...well, I'd known since we were talking earlier. Besides, there's been gossip about Kazuki's ring ever since he started school."

"You...knew...?"

The stress suddenly lessened all at once, and Wataru unthinkingly spoke in a lifeless voice. It certainly wasn't strange for Masanobu to have noticed given how long they'd been with him.

"Huh...but then, Kazuki..."

"Yeah. He seems shrewd. Maybe he already knew I'd noticed the rings. So, I think he was at least prepared for when it'd come to this."

"'Prepared'?"

"Naturally, for everyone to find out about you two. As proof of that, he wasn't especially trying to hide his ring, and I don't suppose he said anything to you?

"No way... "

Kazuki just might do something like that.

Wataru puzzled over this, and couldn't say anything else. Masanobu's opinion seemed to be on-target thus far. If that were the case, how unsightly must he seem in Yuichi's eyes as he tried to hide his own ring?

"I think uprightness is a virtue of his."

The silent Wataru was all of a sudden wrapped up in the gentle tone of voice. When he looked up feebly, Masanobu gave him a nod full of playfulness.

"That you panicked was quite an ordinary reaction. No one exposes their privacy to people they don't know well. That's especially true when it's about love."

"Asaka..."

"Of course, those guys are my club mates and you can trust them. But, you just met them for the first time and I know full-well that you tried to protect Kazuki."

"Did I...really...?"

"It was brave, in my book."

"......"

It seemed mysterious.

Every time Masanobu said something, Wataru's heart was released from unrest and impatience. This sensation was something he'd felt a lot while talking to Yuichi. There was no doubt in what they said, and the sincere sounds gave Wataru a pleasant sense of courage. Even if the words they chose differed, there may have been something fundamentally similar about Yuichi and Masanobu.

"Now, we'd better hurry up with shopping. Sorry to get you involved, Wataru, but could you help out?"

"S...Sure."

Masanobu looked at the again-cheerful Wataru and started walking as if relieved. While following after, Wataru quietly took off his ring.

Wha...

At that instant, his heart ached a little.

However, he didn't bother to think deeply about where it had come from.

"...was a bad idea." muttered Yuichi.

It was thirty minutes after they'd left Masanobu and the others, so at first Wataru had no idea what he was talking about.

"What was a bad idea?   Oh, you mean going shopping earlier? But when I tried challenging the idea of Japanese food for dinner, you..."

"Who's talking about food?"

"Eh...but..."

"I mean Asaka, of course."

As Yuichi said the name with obvious distaste, he shifted the grocery bags in both his hands over to his left, and took his key out the pocket of his cotton pants.

"No 'buts,' he's too focused on you. And he went out of his way to hold your hand, damn it."

"But, that was..."

"I know.   Your ring was off when you came back. But it's not Asaka's place to bail you out."

"That's true...but..."

"You're your own person."

The apartment door was opened roughly and Wataru was urged to go in first. Seeing that Yuichi's mood was rather foul, Wataru removed his sneakers without opposing him.

I had a feeling... I didn't think I'd get by without him saying anything...

They'd planned to make dinner together as always, so most of the food had been bought. Wataru put it temporarily on the dining table and waited dejectedly for Yuichi.

Well, I guess it's no wonder he got mad...

Even so, had he been holding it in until they got back to the apartment? That day he had declared to Wataru that "I don't raise my voice on the street." He must have wanted to get mad, but couldn't.

That kind of thing's cute about him, though.

Knowing when he muttered this that it would only pour oil on Yuichi's fire, Wataru entered the kitchen silently and with a sullen look on his face.

"H-Hey, Kazuki? I'm really sorry about what happened. But Asaka did that out of goodwill, so don't be so..."

"He took your hand and walked out in front of everyone, but because it was in goodwill, I should just let it go?"

Saying this, Yuichi threw food into the refrigerator in anger. When Wataru sighed, secretly wondering when dinner would be ready at this rate, Yuichi's hands suddenly stopped moving as if he was tired.

"Kazuki...what is it...?"

"...So, does it bother you?"

"Does what...bother me?"

"You know, the rings."

"Eh...!... "

Now that Yuichi had gradually hit upon the core of the conversation, Wataru faltered at once. However, as if this had produced a false misunderstanding, Yuichi closed the refrigerator door weakly with a depressed look on his face.

"It's true... Things are different than they were in high school."

"Kazuki... "

"They were the 'in thing' then, and everyone wore them for fun. So, no matter how much our rings looked alike, no one would be truly suspicious of our relationship."

"......"

"But now the situation's different. Even I know that in my head. Of course, it would hurt your feelings for complete strangers to look at you with eyes full of curiosity. I never want you to have to deal with that. But..."

Yuichi stopped speaking, and bit his lip out of frustration. Even though he wanted to blame Wataru for disappearing with Masanobu, he couldn't by any means do so. His painful vexation was communicated, and Wataru rushed to embrace him.

"I'm sorry, Kazuki. Sorry..."

"Wataru... "

"I panicked. I thought for sure you'd be in trouble if the matching ring was spotted. You've just started college, and I don't know what kind of people are there. Then Asaka sent me a lifeboat. I thought it was mean to do to you, but Asaka understood. So...you can talk badly about me, but leave Asaka out of it. Even he saw what you were prepared to do. He didn't look at us strangely even after he knew the truth. So...I'm sorry..."

"......"

His cheek against his warm chest, Wataru repeated "I'm sorry" over and over. Yuichi seemed bewildered by the intensity at first, but before long he slowly reached out his right hand and pulled Wataru's head up to his.

"Enough talk about Asaka."

"Kazuki..."

"Geez. This is nothing for you to apologize over..."

The fingers combing through his hair were radiating points of warmth. He couldn't see his expression, but from the warm breath coming down on him, Wataru felt the atmosphere calm bit by bit.

"You're not just slow, you're a fool, too."

Yuichi murmured with an extremely sweet tone.

"What I got mad about was...just..."

"Just...?"

"I just didn't like the fact that it was Asaka who got you to take your ring off. If you were going to take it off anyway, I wish it'd been me."

He seemingly spat that out as he held Wataru tightly. The suffocating strength behind it must have been the awkwardness of expressing his true feelings.

"Kazuki... I'm sorry..."

In Yuichi's arms, Wataru cast his eyes downward with a hint of throbbing pain. It was the pain he'd felt when he took the ring off. Now, he finally understood the reason.

",Wataru, hold out your left hand."

"Huh...?"

After holding each other in silence for a while, Yuichi abruptly slackened the strength in his arms and spoke. The left hand, timidly extended, held his quiet gaze.

Yuichi opened his mouth without even blinking.

"From now on, I'll leave it up to your discretion."

"My discretion...?"

"Yeah. When you wear the ring, and when you take it off. That way, we're not fighting over it every single time. We should've learned from when we lost this ring once, we can't be preoccupied with appearances alone."

"Yeah...but..."

"It's okay. More importantly, the way Asaka casually touched you is what gets me. I bet he was watching you before at the café, too."

The moment he realized Yuichi had noticed, Wataru's whole body felt hot. He had a feeling that Masanobu's stare had seen straight into his heart as it unsettled him.

"Got it, Wataru?"

Yuichi drew his left hand towards him forcefully and kissed it on the palm. It was a long, long kiss, like it was filled with a wish.

"Kazuki...uh..."

"Look me in the eye."

"......"

"Because I'm looking you in yours."

Yuichi spoke forcefully, with upturned eyes so clear they were enchanting.

Wataru couldn't find the words to answer with, and all he could do was nod quietly.

It was three days later when Wataru found out that Yuichi had decided on a job.

Just when Wataru had finished class and was taking out his cell phone to contact Yuichi, as if it was magically timed, a voice mail came in. What's more, all that was said was "I picked a job." It didn't touch on details at all, and simply ended with "I'll call you again tonight." Wataru hurriedly sent a reply message, but maybe he was busy because a response didn't come back.

"So now you've got too much time on your hands."

"Well, Kazuki cancelled at the last minute. Truth be told, we had arranged to have dinner at his apartment and I was going straight there after school..."

Wataru's little sister Karin, who'd been making dinner, looked down at him half-sprawled on the dining room table. Like his close friend Kawamura, she was one of the few people who knew that Wataru and Yuichi fell in love, so Wataru was able to be openly sad in front of her.

"It's okay, once in a while. You haven't been home at all lately, Wataru. Be thankful you can partake of my cooking today!"

"I'll bet you spend tons of time at Toko's store every break you get. I heard this from Kazuki, but you're learning how to engrave from her? That's a bit unexpected."

"Ha ha, you found out? Toko promised that in the future, when I can do it well, she'll give me a job. Then, in place of her, I'll make new rings for you two. Look forward to it!"

"Rings for us? You will?"

"Sure. I've actually been thinking I'd like to make accessories and such, and you and Kazuki are what did it."

Karin said all of this unexpectedly while tasting the miso soup. When Wataru lifted his head to look at her, he got an embarrassed-looking smile in return.

"You know, it was actually those rings that brought you two together. Looking at them, I thought...wouldn't it be great if I could make little things that a person could convey his feelings with that way? Wouldn't that be fantastic?"

"Karin..."

"So, also as thanks to both of you, I'll make some really good ones. Well, just be patient. Toko's a pretty strict teacher."

"Okay...good luck."

Toko was Yuichi's cousin, and also the woman who made the ring Wataru was currently wearing. Apparently during her big brother's love drama, Karin and Toko had found a lot in common with each other.

Karin had taken charge of housework since both parents had jobs, and she had really come a long way in some areas for a year's time. Because of her temperament, she probably wouldn't just aspire and plan her dream. Wataru reacted to suddenly realizing his little sister's growth with surprise and at the same time deep emotion.

"And now Kazuki's started a job... I shouldn't be the only one sitting around."

"Speaking of which, what job did he get? This is Kazuki, so whatever it is it's probably not simply explained."

"Yeah, you've got a point..."

Pouting his lips like it was difficult to say, Wataru feebly rested his chin in his hands. Compared to Karin cheerfully talking about future dreams, it must have looked like he was sulking over a trivial thing. But even though the patheticness of it hit him, it didn't make the answer any more interesting.

"He won't...tell me."

"Huh?"

"He sent me a text message saying 'I picked a job'…and there's been no response since. I think he'll probably call me, but..."

"What, you're sulking over that?"

He was easily laughed at now. Wataru had less and less ground to stand on.

"Sorry I took so long, Wataru."

Lying on his bed, Wataru reflexively let out

a short sigh at the voice pouring into his ear. It was because he had had his cell with him while cleaning up after dinner and taking a bath, waiting for Yuichi to call. He loved Yuichi's voice so much, it canceled out all that worry with just one sentence.

But, today he couldn't adopt a nice attitude right away. Wataru stiffened his mouth sullenly, and Yuichi soon spoke again.

"Wataru? Come on, at least answer."

"Well, what's your job? Is that why you got home late? It's already eleven..."

"Yeah, it's that late already. Maybe because it was the first day, my sense of time's thrown off. Sorry."

"So, what's this job you got?"

Quite unable to get the pertinent info from him, Wataru became a little irritated. Maybe it was his imagination, but he sensed a faint hesitation before the reply from the other end of the phone.

"Kazuki, what's going on?"

"Yeah. It'd take a while to go into detail, so I'll just sum up for now. You know that house Asaka led us to the other day?"

"House...the one being remodeled..."

"Yeah. Actually, I'm going to help out with the remodeling for two or three weeks."

"Oh...then, you joined his circle?"

"No, it's not that."

Surprising Wataru by answering no, Yuichi began explaining the course of events in a cautious tone.

"It's simply a part-time job. Asaka asked me if

I'd help them out as a job instead of joining the circle. It was a pretty good-paying job for such a short time, so...I hesitated, but ended up accepting. He must have been looking through the help-wanted mag I left behind. He considerately offered a high hourly rate based on the job openings I'd checked off."

"Asaka did...?"

The instant he heard Masanobu's name, Wataru felt his heart beat harder. He hadn't heard Yuichi say Masanobu's name since what happened, so it somehow made him feel uncomfortable.

"Wataru…"

Yuichi called his name reservedly. It was a voice like he could totally see Wataru's expression. Not knowing why his pulse had sped up, Wataru asked "Eh...?" in return.

"Kazuki...d'you say something?"

"I'm going to be going straight from lecture to helping out there for a while. If you feel like coming to hang out you can. Spectators are welcome, after all."

"You sure? But...wouldn't I be in the way?"

It was many times better then being told not to come, but he figured he would try being reserved. Yuichi laughed weakly, but all he responded with was a short "It's cool."

"Part-time job...huh..."

Even after the call ended, Wataru held the cell in his hand and pondered absentmindedly for a while.

"If he's paying him money, Asaka must really want to win Kazuki over into his group."

It's not as if Wataru didn't honestly wonder

why Masanobu would go that far, but there might have been circumstances involved that he didn't know about. Though, if he went to see Yuichi, he would inevitably run into Masanobu. The fact that he had been the point of their argument before made Wataru wear a troubled frown.

"I do think that Asaka is a good person..."

It was brave, in my book, he could still hear his kind voice murmur in his ears. If he'd heard that exchange, Yuichi's reaction might have been very different.

"What's the deal here...?"

He sighed very deeply, and the cell rang again. He looked surprisedly at the LCD, and mail from Yuichi showed up.

"Good night, Wataru.   See you again tomorrow."

"Kazuki... "

His heart suddenly got light and warm.

This was the first time the words "See you again tomorrow" had ever made him this happy. Yuichi had implied "I'll be waiting." Wataru had been worrying about this-and-that so much he'd racked his brain. That one short sentence had been packed with tons of Yuichi's affection.

"Good night, Kazuki...see you tomorrow."

While smiling, Wataru instinctively and politely responded by saying the same.

The next school day finally ended.

Beneath his calm surface, Wataru still had some reservations, but he decided to visit Yuichi's workplace.

"Well, leave it to me. I'll take care of those college girls there who look like they'll get in the way of your romance!"

"Kawamura, I think you have the wrong idea..."

"Why? Isn't that why you invited me?"

"That has nothing to do with it."

Listening to Kawamura's joking offer made Wataru's seriousness seem silly. Even though the ring-wearing boom had long since died down, Kawamura was the only one still looking for a partner to share rings with.

They took trains from school for about thirty minutes, and then got off at the same street at the date the other day. Since Yuichi had started working, they'd had to put their daytime plans on hold for a while, but it was for money for their trip, so it couldn't be helped. Wataru was absent-mindedly thinking over their new schedule.

"Oh? If it isn't Wataru."

"Ah, Asaka... H...Hello."

As Wataru and Kawamura turned off the street down the alley, Masanobu suddenly spoke to them. They turned around and there he was, smiling and wearing work clothes stylishly, like they were brand-name. Kawamura wore a bewildered expression from seeing Masanobu's face.

"You're here to see Kazuki?"

"Th-That's right. Uh, I really want to thank you for the other day!"

Wataru hurriedly bowed his head, but Yuichi's face came to mind at once, and he wasn't able to go on. Masanobu answered "You're welcome" smilingly, not seeming to pay any attention.

"You have a friend with you today? Kazuki's already working inside."

"I see...okay..."

"What's up?"

Masanobu spoke through a wry smile while peering at Wataru who was avoiding eye contact. Then he thumped him on his head, and, as if incidentally, pulled lightly on his left earlobe.

"Wh-What are you doing?!"

"Ah, you finally looked up. You must be worried about something. I thought maybe you were mad at me."

"Why would I be mad at you?"

"Because I dragged Kazuki into this job. It's only for a short time, but it's hard work. I think it'll be tough for him when he's not used to it. And he'll have no time for dates."

Having spouted his quick-witted lines at the drop of a hat, Masanobu grinned once again. He turned to Kawamura, who'd been looking wary for some time now, and sought to make sure. "You do know, right?"

"Uh...oh, yes..."

"Yeah. I figured you were safe since Wataru brought you all this way. Well, I'm heading back in. See you later."

Raising his right hand a bit, Masanobu started walking. Watching the well-postured retreating figure,

Kawamura spoke bitingly and quickly.

"Who the heck is he? Is this a habit of yours now?"

"Well, he's Kazuki's upperclassman... What are you talking about, 'habit'?"

"I mean, that guy looks a lot like Kazuki. Why do unusual types like that only show up around you?"

"Looks like...Kazuki...?"

Reflexively, Wataru raised his voice. He'd certainly associated Masanobu's bearing with Yuichi, but he resisted the assertion that they resembled each other.

"Maybe...he does. I mean, Kazuki isn't the take-charge type like Asaka, and he's not that cheerful..."

"Whoa, whoa, what planet are you on?"

"Huh?"

"In high school Kazuki was totally the same type. Even if he didn't do club activities, he was constantly helping out somewhere. He was highly popular with both underclassmen and teachers, and nice to everyone. Well, actually he was outrageously perverse."

"......"

Hearing it put that way, Wataru couldn't even answer. When they first met, Yuichi was the embodiment of the honor student and the object of everyone's admiration. Even as the only one who saw his unkindness, Wataru, had to admit how cool he was.

As Wataru brooded over his complex feelings, Kawamura dug into him all the more.

"Overall, there's something odd about you."

"Odd? About me?"

"That's right. You just let him touch your head and ear. Are you that kind of guy? Isn't that bad?"

"Ughh, shut up."

Wataru countered his friend's frank opinion with an awkward rebuttal. Masanobu's actions were so natural, he felt like if he resisted awkwardly he'd get so self-conscious he'd be laughed at.

"Well, whatever. Ah, isn't that the place?"

The place he'd spotted was right in front of them. Incited by subject-changing Kawamura, Wataru walked through the open sliding door with a head full of puzzled thoughts.

"Wow, the inside's totally different from the outside."

Kawamura muttered quietly after looking around fully at the surroundings.

"It's like they're making an exhibit for a culture festival or something. Seriously, students are doing all of this?"

"It looks that way. I was surprised too when Kazuki was invited to work here, but maybe they need that much help."

"So, where's Kazuki? You know, the reason we came?

Careful of the lumber and carpentry tools scattered around their feet, they slowly made their way further in. There were even less people there than the last time, and they only saw two girls with paint brushes in the courtyard.

"That what's his name, Asaka, isn't around either."

"Yeah...eh?"

Wataru had reached the center of the floor, and suddenly noticed a small room off to the right. It was originally where the kitchen was, and was divided off by the lone remaining first-floor wall. He thought he heard multiple voices coming from it.

He tried to call out to Kawamura, but he'd started talking to the college girls in the courtyard and was cheerily making his way in their direction. With nothing else to do, Wataru softly made his way towards the voices so as not to disturb their conversation.

"...Kazuki. If you put a nail in it there, the mirror on the front will develop cracks easily. Be careful."

"Oh, sorry."

"It's an application of physics, so think of it with those calculations you're good at. You're good at science and math, right?"

"I'll redo it."

Speaking extremely patiently, Yuichi was getting advice from Masanobu while wrestling with what was apparently a full-length mirror. Maybe because the frame was adorned with decorations, it looked hard to work with.

Kazuki...

Where had the usual cool expression disappeared to? Wataru had never seen him looking so into something, and he couldn't bring himself to carelessly say anything.

Kazuki, why...?

Unintentionally choked up, Wataru couldn't help but ask that question in his heart.

Perhaps the mirror was slated to decorate the gallery. Yuichi was earnestly trying to affix the metal fixtures for attaching it to a wall. But Masanobu had corrected him so many times it was evident that he was steadily losing his composure.

Because...because I can't work part-time.

Wataru continued to gaze at Yuichi while dealing with bitter emotions. It was definitely Yuichi who said they should go on a trip. But Wataru never imagined he would have to work a hard job he wasn't good at for that reason.

"I hesitated, but ended up accepting."

Last night Yuichi had said that falteringly. He'd been upset that Masanobu had led Wataru away, and maybe he never really wanted a job in the first place. The reason he'd done it at all was for the expense of the trip.

"Kazuki, Wataru's here."

Masanobu suddenly pointed at him. Yuichi raised his head from the mirror, looked at Wataru, and adopted a dejected look. For an instant Wataru lost his nerve, but Masanobu spoke up first.

"Wataru, come on in. I was just thinking of taking a little break."

"But..."

"Why do you look depressed? Oh, did you think I was being mean to Kazuki?"

"I, I didn't think that!"

"Then come in. Want some canned coffee?"

Beckoned in enthusiastically, Wataru nervously approached them. When he glanced at Yuichi, he was wiping dirt off his cheek with the back of his hand and opening his mouth to say "You know..."

"I bet you've just been standing there.   That makes me nervous, so just come in immediately."

"Sorry."

Seeing Wataru was downhearted, Yuichi's eyes suddenly softened. Wataru felt a little relieved when his original expression returned.

"Here, your coffee. Oh? You took yours off today, too?"

"Eh...?"

"I guess you both decided? Well, there might be less to worry about that way."

For a moment Wataru couldn't really tell what Masanobu was talking about. But he was taken aback when he shifted his gaze to Yuichi's hands and the glittering ring that should have been there wasn't. His heart began pounding violently.

"K-Kazuki...uh..."

"I didn't want to damage it."

"Eh...that's all...?"

"Of course it is. There's no other reason for me to have to take it off."

In any case, Yuichi's answer seemed to be aimed at Masanobu. Wataru at once felt ashamed at the sound of that deliberate voice.

"Pretty contradictory, for you not wearing your own."

"Ugh..."

Was it his imagination, or did Yuichi smile? Maybe it made him happy that Wataru's face was so serious. But as Masanobu was right next to him, he suddenly hid his smile in a sour look.

"You two sure are cute."

Masanobu chuckled and flashed a smile, with something like nostalgia in his eyes.

"C-Cute...? Asaka..."

"Ahh, sorry. I didn't mean it in a bad way. It's just, your faces are so different when you're together than when you're not. Kazuki is a different person. He has a more grown-up feel when I see him on campus..."

"It's your prerogative to act like my superior, but would you mind laying off the two of us?"

Yuichi spat the words out roughly, in a harsh voice. Masanobu cheerfully shrugged his shoulders like he'd paid it no mind, and whispered not to Yuichi, but to Wataru, "Sorry, y'know?"

"Kazuki..."

Wataru hissed in a thoroughly disgusted voice to Yuichi, who was sitting opposite him.

"This place really doesn't suit you."

"What's that supposed to mean?"

"You've been totally on-edge since that moment."

"That's not my fault."

Yuichi made his retort calmly while crossing his legs. But the waitress who had shown them to their table was obviously walking on air, and from here and there lots of heated glances were being directed his way. It was definitely because Yuichi's refined good looks stood out strongly in the mundane atmosphere of the family restaurant.

Maybe because of the annoying stares, Yuichi spoke again with a sullen frown.

"Are you sure we shouldn't have invited your friend? What's his name, Kawasaki..."

"Kawamura.   Just   remember   it   already, Kazuki."

"He didn't seem interested in being around me."

Wataru smiled ruefully at Yuichi's justified statement.   When they parted ways, Kawamura was quite hyped up about having dinner with a "college girl" he'd hit it off with.

"...So."

Yuichi spoke without smiling, eyes pointed down at the menu in his hands.

"Why are we here in a family restaurant? Weren't we supposed to go have dinner at my apartment?"

"Well...you know, you're always cooking.   I thought we could eat out now and then..."

"You've got something to say to me, don't you?"

"...Yeah."

Of course, his poor lie didn't work on Yuichi. Even so, Wataru still felt some hesitation, but he resolutely opened his mouth.

"I was...thinking, maybe I should stop coming to see you at work."

"Why?"

"I mean...it's in everyone's way... Asaka is nice about it, but it's your job and you seem busy. I'd just be a bother..."

"Wataru, say what you really mean."

Yuichi was getting irritated.

"If you were a bother, I wouldn't have invited you in the first place. You know that at least, don't you? I have to work weekends too, and we won't have time to take it easy for a while, so I invited you."

"But...I can't stay there..."

"Can't stay there?"

It seemed that, to Yuichi, this was an unforeseen response. Looking downward, Wataru searched with all his might for the words to explain it well.

"...To tell you the truth I found it all pretty strange. Why you'd agree to take Asaka's job when he annoys you so much? I mean, it might pay well, but it looked really rough in there today. Being made to redo that so many times by him..."

"So what? You saw an unbecoming side of me, and now you're disillusioned or something?"

"That not it!"

Wataru raised his voice in anger, his head coming up.

"I'm the unbecoming one. The...only you I've ever known is the one who can handle anything with ease. This was the first time I'd ever seen you at a loss...and it made me ashamed of myself when I had just come to be a casual observer."

"......"

"You're human too, Kazuki. Of course you'd be bewildered by work you weren't used to. I'd forgotten something even that basic. I couldn't stand that about myself. I'd meant to understand everything about you after being with you for almost a year...but then, Asaka..."

"Asaka what?"

Yuichi had been listening quietly, but he reacted sharply to Masanobu's name.

"This is between you and me. Why did Asaka's name come up all of a sudden?"

"He's on our side, isn't he? You don't have to refer to him that way."

"Wataru..."

"He said that you're a different person when you're with me, didn't he? I thought, that might not be a good thing. If you paid all your attention to me, someone not in the group, it'd be hard even for you to work with the others. Then, I would end up being a nuisance in the end...so..."

I want to see you, but maybe it'd be best to just wait. That's what he wanted to say, but Wataru couldn't bring himself to say it.

"...Wataru."

After a short silence, Yuichi murmured softly.

"You want to see me, don't you?"

"Yeah... "

"I said this before. I don't care if it's five minutes or one, you can call me anytime. Can I hope for the same from you now?"

"Kazuki..."

"Besides, I don't want to quit this job. I'll bet Asaka would laugh at me if I quit now. That's one thing I won't have."

"Asaka would laugh? At you?"

For whatever reason, Wataru parroted Yuichi's words as he asked in return. It was because Masanobu really didn't seem like the type of person to ridicule others.

"It doesn't mean Asaka's mean."

Yuichi smiled bitterly.

"It's only our second day working together, but he's definitely a great guy. For being so suave, what he says and does always puts others first. In the first place, the way he arranged for me to be paid was thanks to the fact that he's got a great relationship with the owner. I have to wonder how he twisted his words around for that one..."

"He went that far to get you?"

"Yeah.   My face, brains, and personal connections."

"Personal connections..."

"I hadn't told you, but my older brother is an architect. He supervised the plans for the remodeling Asaka is helping out with.   So...with my relatives dragged into it, if something came up he could easily deal with it. Even without that, a project like this one always goes through change after change. They are, after all, a group of amateurs.

"So...that's the case..."

He got the feeling that one part of the mystery was finally solved. Yuichi maintained a disinterested tone the entire time, like he was trying as much as possible not to express his personal feelings.

"The good thing about Asaka is how he doesn't have some nasty underlying motive. He's probably the kind of person you sense he is, Wataru. Otherwise, even you probably wouldn't get that look on your face in front of him."

"What look on my face...?"

"It's unconscious, so you have trouble managing it."

While what he'd just said seemed to have deep meaning, Yuichi didn't appear about to explain any further than that. After yawning like he was tired, he spoke again out-of-the-blue.

"I don't like Asaka."

"Huh...?"

"It's been awkward with him ever since he first spoke to me once I started school. But, it's not like he's to blame. Like I said before, Asaka's a well-made guy. So...I've come to want to know why exactly."

"Kazuki?"

"I decided it when he was covering for you and then walked off…that I'd find out. You know, what it is about Asaka that makes me anxious, what irritates me, that's what I want to confirm. So, I went along with the job idea. I'd had enough of running from him, anyway."

This was perhaps the first time that strong emotion had arisen in Yuichi. His looks and talent weren't the only reasons why he'd been loved by everyone around him.

Yuichi was a very kind guy, and Wataru knew that better than anyone. He was a person who always considered the other person's feelings, and he could play the part he was needed to play.

Now, he was embracing rare negative feelings towards Masanobu. Wataru knew well that he was perplexed by this fact.

"You feel at ease when Asaka's around, don't you?"

"Eh?"

"I could see it on your face. But that's bad how it's unconscious. Earlier I..."

"Excuse me... What would you like to order...?"

The waitress had been quite unable to interrupt the conversation, but she spoke up as if she'd found the resolve. Yuichi glanced at her, and slowly got up from his seat.

"K-Kazuki! Where're you going?!"

"I said too much. Sorry, I'm going home."

"Wait up a minute!"

Wataru hurriedly tried to stop him, but the left hand he started to reach out with was instead grabbed. Yuichi let an expressionless gaze fall on the bare ring finger, then he quickly released Wataru's hand.

"Kazuki..."

"Later, Wataru."

Waving his right hand, Yuichi headed for the door without even turning around. Left behind, Wataru stood half-dumbfounded as he silently watched him walk away.

It was now one week later.

With his ring tucked into the breast pocket of

his uniform, Wataru went to see Yuichi as much as time would allow.

Because the day's work would sometimes extend well into the night, there were many days when he couldn't hang out until the end, but even so Wataru continued to come by.

"Wataru, you're really everyone's idol."

Masanobu said that to tease him, but in actuality Wataru had felt bad just watching and undertook odd jobs like errand and shopping. Thanks to this, everyone had affectionately started calling him "Junior."

"You're a big help to us."

Masanobu offered this with an apologetic air, while drinking the juice Wataru had bought in the kitchen with him.

"Aren't you bored, not being able to take your time talking to Kazuki even though you came all the way here?"

"Well...this is a workplace, so I can't help that. Besides, I know Kazuki's gradually warming up to the job, so I don't want to bother him."

"Yeah, I knew he had good intuition. He's quick to grasp things, so everyone thinks he's useful. To-date, he's even had display ideas."

"Is that so..."

Yuichi hasn't told me a thing about that. Our unpleasant parting at the restaurant must have had a lasting effect, after all.

At the moment, Yuichi was in the gallery taking to club members about where to put the big mirror. Wataru could see him distantly, but it was too far for his voice to carry. Sadly, there was a sense of such a distance between them widening day-by-day.

"Uh, is this okay, Asaka?"

"Is what?"

"You being occupied with me. Aren't you with me every time Kazuki seems busy? And you explain to me about what everyone is doing."

"Well, PR is part of my job."

Masanobu answered readily, always with that smile that made Wataru feel relieved. In actuality, the times he took part in real work were extremely few, and he was usually on the phone with someone or off to a meeting, so there were many moments where he'd simply be drinking tea with Wataru.

"But, it's like everyone's relying on you one way or another. You really do feel like the leader here..."

Even while he was saying that, a college guy carrying some plans walked up to Masanobu. The two of them had an exchange of technical terms that Wataru didn't understand, and Masanobu started briefly drawing other lines on the plans with the red pen he'd been holding. When he saw his direct hand movements and serious profile, Wataru was unintentionally fascinated by him.

He's so cool, Wataru thought for the hundredth time.

The width of the gap between when he was chatting and when he was working made Masanobu's depth of character very clear.

I wonder if Yuichi's found his own answer, working together with Masanobu.

"As for what we're doing here..."

Seeing Wataru's lost expression, Masanobu often told him about what they were working on in an easily understandable way.

"You could say it's a game to see how effectively we can reuse the existing building. So, arranging things in a modern way while destroying as little flavor of the building itself becomes the theme."

"Then, it's like the current fad of remaking old clothes."

"Right, right. The construction version of that. This time, it's for use as a gallery, so the interior's somewhat predetermined. Among other things, the big mirror Kazuki was fighting hard with the other day and the shelves the girls are setting up over there are all items to be used for display. Since the exhibits are going to be pop art, I said they might as well turn the entire room into a toy box."

"Uhuh... I was thinking everyone would make even the exhibits together. It looked like something completely different than regular carpentry work."

"Yeah, it might look that way to an observer. My job is to raise money for the budget and oversee the overall balance, so I'm trying as much as possible not to micromanage. I'm perfectionist by nature, so if I got involved in any one job, wouldn't I lose objectivity in overseeing the whole project?"

Like it was as easy as playing, Masanobu always looked into everyone's situation. Because of this, no matter what someone came to him with, chances are he could deal with it immediately. Besides, the uniquely calm air about him had the mysterious effect of calming the scene as well. In a place where people with strong personalities worked together, it was perhaps an invaluable talent.

"Wataru?   Sorry, but could you do some shopping?"

"Eh...?"

At some point while Wataru had been listening in admiration to Masanobu, Yuichi had suddenly appeared. Wataru stood up hurriedly and looked back at him all in a flutter. Even though it was unavoidable, being seen having a friendly chat with Masanobu when Yuichi had stated he didn't like him made Wataru feel awkward inside.

"S...Sure. What am I buying?"

"We're about to run out of blue and brown paint. No one has their hands free at the moment."

"Isn't that too much for one person? I'll go along with him."

"Asaka..."

"If we both go, we can get enough to keep a reserve. We were just now having a good time over tea anyway."

Speaking like he'd been caught somehow, Masanobu slowly got to his feet. Yuichi didn't say anything, but he didn't try to hide the displeased color that entered his eyes.

"Asaka. This is bad for me."

"What is?"

"Please don't say things that irritate Kazuki. If

you do..."

"He doesn't like me, does he?"

With a matter-of-fact face, Masanobu got down to the point. They were on their way back, paint cans hanging from every hand.

"In any case, whatever I do, I don't think he's going to like me."

"That couldn't be... "

"You haven't noticed? When you and I are talking, he pays lots of attention to us. He pretends he's indifferent as much as he can, but I'm sensitive to things like that."

You're kidding, Wataru almost said without thinking, but closed his mouth in a panic. The moment Masanobu spelled it out, Wataru started fretting.

"I'm not kidding."

Seeing right through him, Masanobu smiled once more.

"You looked offended because you don't notice at all. If it makes you mad, let it come out more openly in your attitude. That's why I wanted to be a little mean to you."

"So that's why..."

"Maybe it'd be better for you not to have this strange reserve, but indulge more. Wataru, you're too attentive to the needs of others. It's best to use false courage as little as possible."

Sometimes Masanobu says the same things as Yuichi. They really are alike, like Kawamura said, thought Wataru.

They finally got back to the house, and went

through the sliding door with a sense of relief. But the instant they got inside, their ears were met with a stormy, shouting voice. They put the paint cans on the floor and hurried towards the gallery.

"Kazuki...?"

There, Wataru stopped.

In the center of a heavy air glaring at each other were Yuichi and another college guy. His agitated counterpart had for some reason been doing all the shouting at Yuichi.

"What's wrong?"

"A-Asaka..."

At Masanobu's appearance, the girl who spoke up was visibly relieved.

"Uh, the display shelf Kobayashi was making doesn't match up with the mirror Kazuki put in. The sizes seem to be off, so they don't line up in the same place."

"So, I'm saying we should take out his mirror. Without a shelf, we can't display the exhibits. It shouldn't even require thought to see which one's the priority. And you're just a part-timer in the first place."

Maybe because Yuichi wasn't losing his cool demeanor at all, Kobayashi seemed to be getting steadily angrier. Everything he kept complaining about gradually sounded more and more like false accusations.

Masanobu kept quiet and watched the scene for a while, but at length he spoke up in quite a light tone.

"Which one is the wrong size?"

"The shelf."

"Then Kobayashi, let's remake the shelf

together. Any way you look at it, making the mirror smaller is beyond our skills. Sorry, but give us a break on this one."

"But...that's easy for you to say now..."

"It's all right. The second time will go faster because you know the process. Everyone pictured the shelf and mirror as a set anyway. If we lose either one, the balance will be off. If that happens, you won't be rewarded for your trouble, will you?"

"No...well..."

Masanobu's voice was constantly light and gentle. Maybe that's why, when you heard that sound pleasant to the ears, you'd be willing to remake something any number of times. The girl who'd been asked a while ago about the situation whispered "There it is, the Asaka magic" into another girl's ear, but Wataru picked it up.

"You know, when I hear Asaka talk, I get a feeling like I could make anything. Really, how many times has he gotten us with that?"

"But, he actually gets the job done."

"He has a strange way of relaxing people."

Their whispered conversation seemed like it was true all right. As proof, Kobayashi was starting to calm down before their eyes. That's when everyone figured the coast was clear and started going back to their own places.

"I don't agree."

The cold voice chilled the atmosphere again just as it started to calm down.

Yuichi, who had held his silence until then,

rejected the assistance. He spoke to Kobayashi without batting an eye in a way that sounded like he'd been set adrift.

"If you're redoing it, please take care of mounting the mirror as well. I have other things to work on, too. Your mistake is what ate time up, so I leave the rest to you."

"Wh-Who do you think you are?"

"I checked things time and again. I asked if the mirror should go here. I thought you and Asaka had both given your consent. I don't think it's funny to suddenly be told categorically that the size is wrong, and have my work interrupted."

Whatever Kobayashi would shout, whatever suggestion Masanobu would bring up, Yuichi fell back into silence. Regretting the fact he was an outsider, Wataru anxiously watched the three of them.

Yuichi should have naturally been able to salvage the situation without making it worse. But now that he's gone and purposefully aggravated things, there must have been some other cause…

"If this is going to drag on any further, I'll just go home for the day. It's not like I'd get any more work done."

Seeing that he was getting nowhere with the persistently argumentative Kobayashi, Yuichi abruptly ended the conversation himself. Masanobu didn't even try to stop him, and he walked directly over to Wataru. It seemed he'd noticed him even amidst all the commotion.

"Kazuki, uh…"

"We're leaving, Wataru."

"Eh?"

Taking Wataru's hand roughly, Yuichi pulled with all his might. Grabbing his own bag from the corner, he headed for the exit without even turning around. Flustered, Wataru desperately searched for the words to make him stop.

"K-Kazuki. You've got to go back..."

"Go back and do what? Get laughed at by them when I'm not the one at fault?"

"That's not what I meant, but this isn't like you. Why'd you pick a fight like that?"

"Not like me?"

Now outside, Yuichi unexpectedly stopped under the totally darkened sky.

"Okay, then what's like me?"

"W-Well..."

"The quiet honor student, always sociable and everyone's peacemaker? We've already got Asaka for that. I'm pissed off."

"Kazuki...could it be...?"

"What?"

"Was it Asaka back there who pissed you off?"

Yuichi turned his head away at Wataru's question. Wataru had confidence in that profile.

"Something's...something's odd, Kazuki. It's really strange!"

"What is?"

"Why do you take everything Asaka says so seriously? I mean, I know you said you don't like him, but he hasn't done anything. I can't believe you'd get so irritated you'd quit your job. You aren't that kind of person, are you?"

"It's not the way I seem, it's the way you acted. Think about it!"

"Me...?"

What the hell is Yuichi talking about? Confused by the sudden words, Wataru just stared back at him.

"Just...because I was talking with Asaka..."

"What, that again?"

Given a look that said "You don't know anything," Wataru got offended once more. Yuichi had been like this whenever the topic of Asaka came up. He might have had something rather deep to say, but he'd never say it.

"Then...why don't you tell me not to come here?! You don't like it when I talk to Asaka, do you?! Then just tell me not to come see you here!"

"Like I said the other day..."

"Then, what should I do? Even if I come here, you're busy. Should I just stare at your face and then go home? Asaka's just looking after me. So I don't get bored..."

"Just looking at my face isn't good enough?"

Yuichi shot him a tight glance. What a thing to say, thought Wataru, but as frustrating as it was, being asked that by a face as truly fair as his was oddly intense and persuasive.

"See, look. You know you love my face."

"Geez, Kazuki..."

"What, Wataru? Say what you want to say."

"You've got a nasty personality."

Glaring with upturned eyes, for an instant Yuichi made a face like he'd been hit through his defenses. But, he soon readopted his cynical-looking smile and said "Thanks for the praise" back to Wataru.

"You can go home now."

"Huh...?"

"There's no way I'm going to quit the job over this. I just got a little worked up. I'll just say sorry to Kobayashi, it's nothing."

"Y-You're joking, right?"

"You want me to skip work? You're the one who said I should go back."

"I did. I did, but..."

"Then don't complain. Later, Wataru."

He spoke quickly, and already had his back turned. At first, Wataru was taken aback, but then turned towards Yuichi in a huff and angrily shouted.

"Stupid jerk! I'm not coming here anymore!"

Yuichi didn't turn around.

He just raised his right hand a waved a little, like at the family restaurant.

"I mean it! Even if you invite me, I won't come here again! I've had enough of you pushing me around!"

Left alone in the dark street for a while, Wataru stood stock still in blank amazement.

Yuichi had long since disappeared through the sliding door.

How long had he been standing there like that?

"Wataru...?"

Softly, someone called out to him. When he raised his head in surprise, Masanobu had been standing in front of him for some amount of time.

"Wataru, are you okay?   I heard shouting voices...oh, that was you?"

"Ah...I'm sorry..."

"No, I was just a little surprised to hear you that way. Besides, that was all Kazuki's angry outburst."

"If it means stuff like this...I wish we hadn't planned the trip..."

Even though he didn't know the situation, Masanobu kept quiet after Wataru said that to himself. I wonder if Yuichi would be in another bad mood if he saw this scene?

"Maybe I'm being wasteful."

"Huh?"

"Because I know Kazuki's trying hard at this job so he can go on a trip with me...I try as hard as I can not to do things that make him unhappy...but, for some reason we keep fighting..."

"Wataru... "

Weakness having unexpectedly come to the surface, Wataru looked away from Masanobu abruptly. He'd risked having a side of him exposed he didn't want to have seen.

"But, you mentioned fighting... Because he's the one you love, you're going to fight, even over irrational things."

"......"

"If I don't, I won't be able to really be equal with him."

Wataru said this firmly, as if telling himself so.

Masanobu started to reach out to Wataru with his right hand, but the usual cheerful touch didn't come this time.

"That's true. I think you're right."

For some reason, as he murmured this with his face upturned to the night sky, he looked even lonelier that Wataru who'd had a fight with his beloved.

"I guess one week was my breaking point, in the end."

As always, Wataru hesitated a short while, standing in front of the run-down house. Even the sliding door, left open during the day, was now closed, and it felt kind of like he was being rejected.

"But, I can't stand here forever... And Kazuki's cell is on voice mail while he's at work."

He muttered to himself outloud, to encourage himself.

Since the night he fought with Yuichi, Wataru hadn't shown up at all. Yuichi had sent rather short update messages, and Wataru had obediently replied to them, but the mood was still far from one of reconciliation.

"...Okay."

This is not a kids' fight, there's no reason to stand here worrying, Wataru told himself, and put his hand on the sliding door. Chances are, Yuichi had been waiting for Wataru to come by every day. But, Yuichi had a rare stubbornness, so it was up to Wataru to cave in on this.

"Oh, it's Junior. Been a while."

"H-Hello."

One of the girls quickly spotted Wataru and spoke up once he walked in. It had only been a week since he'd dropped by, but work on the inside had progressed a surprising amount. The walls were painted a bright cream color, and display shelves of various sizes had been installed on the walls.

"Are you looking for Kazuki?"

Another girl approached while carrying bricks in both hands. Wataru nodded reservedly, and she smiled and pointed to the courtyard.

"Kazuki's there making signs with everyone. He's got an interesting knack for it."

"With...everyone?"

"That's right. He ended up stepping on the first sign we made. There was a big fuss about it then, but that led to him opening up. He has a composure I wouldn't have expected from someone that young, and he's quick-thinking. He's become really popular.

"I see..."

"He even works well with Kobayashi now."

In the courtyard was a bunched-up group of seven or eight men and women, but Yuichi must have been in the center of them. Unfortunately, Wataru wasn't able to spot him.

"So? Want me to go call him?"

Wataru's expression looked a little more depressed, so she adopted a kinder tone.

"If I went now, I'm sure..."

Suddenly, loud laughing voices drowned out her words. Brought back to reality, Wataru was attacked by an unbearable sense of isolation.

"Junior...?"

"I'm sorry, I'll come back again. I don't want to be in the way, and it wasn't especially urgent."

"Oh, but..."

"Thank you very much."

Breaking away from the confused girl, Wataru quickly turned around. In the end, here he was nothing more than Yuichi's "Junior." The proof that he was his boyfriend was sealed in his pocket, and in any case there was no way he'd ever be a real part of their group with his mediocre grades.

He should have been glad when Yuichi came to mind. But he honestly couldn't be. This place was steadily adding to a Yuichi he didn't know. Thinking about that made him feel inescapably lonely.

"Wataru? Where are you going?"

Wataru was about to rush out the sliding door, but he was almost ran smack into Masanobu, who'd just come in. He must have picked up on the unusual atmosphere, because before Wataru could say the first word, Masanobu deftly grasped his shoulder and opened his mouth.

"It's all right."

It was an all-encompassing, tender voice. At times he would show a sharp look in his eyes, but his voice at least was full of a constant amount of kindness.

"It's time we had some good tea."

Saying that, Masanobu drew Wataru's body along with a strength that wouldn't take no for an answer.

An early-blooming hydrangea adorned the table. It was ten minutes before Wataru noticed this, sitting in his seat by the window.

"Do you feel a little better?"

In the opposite seat, Masanobu had a calm smile on his face. As with Yuichi in the restaurant, glances from female customers were focusing his way.

"Try having some tea. This place specializes in Chinese tea, and drinking it really relaxes you.

"Well, all right."

He bobbed his head down slightly and looked at the tea set brought to him especially to help soothe his miserable feelings. A small teapot like someone would play house with and a white teacup for a one-gulp swallow were lined up snugly on the tray.

"It's kind-of strange."

While watching Wataru pour the tea in an awkward manner, Masanobu spoke happily.

"I want to try creating a cafe with my club mates, and I've been searching around for a long time for one that feels right. So, as of now I've found two that I like, and you've been in both of them."

"Does that mean...?"

"Yeah. That classic spot the old couple run and this place. I'm having tea in a place I enjoy with a person I enjoy. It's quite a nice feeling."

"Come on... "

Precisely because he was feeling down, Masanobu's words went straight to his heart one-by-one. They were lines just like those used to woo a girl, but there wasn't a trace of creepiness in his voice.

"Kazuki's warmed up to us, you know?"

Moving on, Masanobu changed the subject to Yuichi. The hot tea and the light chatting made Wataru's loneliness start to melt away.

"To be honest, I didn't think he'd end up getting along that well with everyone. You too, right? That's why you ended up feeling lonely?"

"Asaka... Don't tell me you were watching?"

Wataru unthinkingly blurted this out, even though it couldn't be the case. He was completely taken aback.

"...I didn't actually see Kazuki, but I could hear laughing voices from the courtyard. I figured Kazuki must be who was in the center of the circle, and I suddenly felt like I was all alone. Kazuki is popular but he doesn't like acting out in a group, so I thought he'd just keep quietly to himself for this job..."

"Ahh...yeah, it's mostly individual work, but after all it is a club activity in the end. Our group's especially good together, and there are points where we can't move forward without everyone offering joint opinions."

"That's true. You're the manager, Asaka, so I think everyone has peace of mind. You even console me like this..."

"No, that's because I like you."

Masanobu emphasized it once more, and looked seriously into his eyes.

"You haven't stopped by for about a week now. During that time, you've tried to control your desire to see Kazuki. Despite that, when you got up the courage,

Kazuki seemed to be enjoying himself without you. You could call it bad timing and leave it at that, but it's normal to get angry or pout."

·"Is it...normal...?"

"Of course it is. Take me. I had a girlfriend I saw from middle school into high school. She was very cute, and very selfish. Compared to her, you're so brave it makes me want to cry."

Wataru was a little surprised to hear Masanobu candidly bring up his past. Now that he thought of it, this was the first time he'd talked about himself.

"I am not brave."

Drinking the now-cold tea in one mouthful, Wataru lightly refuted the opinion. Masanobu looked as if he hadn't heard it, and he added, "I envy Kazuki."

"The Wataru I see is always filled to the fingertips with love for him. That presents a bit of a problem."

"Problem..."

"Yes. It's a problem for you to love Kazuki too much."

"Me...?"

What he'd heard was so unexpected, Wataru laughed and tried to shrug it off. But Masanobu's eyes were very serious, and Wataru's laugh stiffened partway through. His directly penetrating gaze held the same heat as the first time it was directed at him.

"Wataru…"

Masanobu spoke without averting his eyes.

"I can't leave you this way."

"Eh..."

"Saying it this way might invite misunderstanding. But, there's no other way to do it."

"What do you mean 'can't leave me this way'...?"

"I'm not really treating you like a child, okay? It's just that when I look at your face I can pretty much tell what you're thinking. When you're sad, you're sad with all your might, and when you're happy it seems to come from the heart. When you look at Kazuki, you make the best face you possibly can. Maybe that's the reason why. Why I care about you blindly."

"Ah, that's right, you like them younger than yourself. As long as they're cute, everyone said..."

"Even I have my own preferences. With cats, for instance, I think shorthaired tigerstripes make good pets. With people, it doesn't matter if they're male or female, I like cuties."

"......"

Maybe this guy doesn't grasp the power his speech has.

It sounded so carefree, Wataru felt amazed inside as he looked back into Masanobu's face.

"Maybe I shouldn't have brought this up."

Perhaps because the silence stretched on, Masanobu seemed to be a little worried. Wataru shook his head in confusion, and timidly opened his mouth."

"Uh...is it bad to love too much?"

"Huh?"

"Before, you said I love Kazuki too much..."

"Ahh...right. Sorry, I didn't mean it negatively. You were just down in the dumps. I was just trying to simply say, positive and negative feelings, they're all born of love."

"......"

"You two have a few more handicaps than typical couples, don't you? So, you have to pay attention to every little chance encounter. But, you can't keep that tension up for too long. Eventually you tire out. Whether your partner is the same sex or not has nothing to do with feelings of love. So, I think it's best to be more laid-back."

"Asaka..."

While listening to him talk, Wataru unconsciously grew to want to sigh.

"Why is it...well, kind-of strange. I feel more cheerful when I'm talking with you. I can't describe it well, but it's like I'm with someone extremely grown-up..."

"Me, a grown-up? For better or for worse, I guess."

Masanobu answered lightly and grinned. All of a sudden, what Kawamura said about him looking like Kazuki vividly came to mind.

Oh, yeah...thought Wataru, like he'd just noticed it.

Perhaps Masanobu reminded him of the "good at relaxing" part of Yuichi, the highly popular, sociable, able-to-handle-anything-you-made-him-do-easily honor student. Yuichi himself had abandoned that face when he got his hands on Wataru, but it had no doubt annoyed him the first time he saw Masanobu. Guys like Masanobu had a great ability to enjoy "their overly good selves."

"I was...wondering why Kazuki gives you a wide berth..."

"That might be a case of likes repelling."

"You already knew?"

"Deep down, we're the same type. But then, as I've been alive two more years, I think I'm more cunning."

Just as Masanobu's voice started sounding more lonely, several people came rushing in noisily. While raising his eyebrows at whatever it was, Wataru shifted his glance to the doorway. It was girls from the club who'd come in, and all their faces were pale.

"Asaka, so this is where you've been!"

"...What's up? Some problem?"

"Kazuki was injured! It looks like that mirror's installation wasn't complete after all... Just as Kazuki was passing in front of it, it collapsed!"

"Say what?"

"We hurried and called a taxi, and sent him to the hospital. He didn't look like he was in much pain, but his left hand was cut and he bled quite a bit, so I'm sure he was toughing through most of it."

"Got it. I'll be back soon."

"Kazuki was... "

Wataru's field of vision swam dizzily. In this warped world, the girls went on talking all the more agitatedly. He got up unsteadily, and drew closer to the nearest one.

"Hospital...where's the hospital...?"

"Behind the station, N General Hospital. He

said he didn't need an escort, and went alone. But, he said he'd call once they were done with first-aid..."

"N General Hospital?"

Without hearing the rest, Wataru flew out of the cafe. Of all things, he was leisurely drinking tea when Yuichi got injured. Intense regret swirled in his chest, but right now he wanted to confirm Yuichi's safety with his own eyes as quickly as possible.

"Kazuki... Kazuki. Kazuki. Kazuki..."

Dashing across the asphalt at full speed, Wataru kept calling Yuichi's name in a delirious ramble.

A shoulder shake woke Wataru up from his shallow snooze. Through his barely open eyes, street lights blurred in the jet blackness.

"Wha..."

It's like I've been dreaming a long time, he thought dimly as he rubbed his eyes. A familiar voice soon murmured near his ears.

"Why're you asleep in front of the door?"

"Ka...zuki...?"

"What happened to the spare key I gave you? You could have gone inside and waited."

"Kazuki!"

His thoughts finally came into focus, and Wataru clung dazedly to Yuichi, who was squatting in front of him. He was too vigorous and inadvertently touched the wound, and Yuichi grimaced slightly, but even so he patted Wataru on the back with his uninjured right hand.

"Geez... I know it's been a while, but talk about

a passionate greeting."

"C-Cut the crap! I went to the hospital when I heard you got hurt...but, I was told that they'd just finished treating you and you'd left, so I tried coming by the apartment..."

"Ahh, sorry. I was worried about the work I left behind, so I went back to the site for a while. Oh yeah, I turned off my cell phone at the hospital and left it that way."

"Don't 'oh yeah' me!"

If Yuichi hadn't been injured, he would have gotten more than that. But now that he'd confirmed his safety, Wataru drew a long sigh of relief.

Since being in the hallway was a neighborhood nuisance, Wataru pulled himself up and went in the apartment. When he inspected it under bright illumination, the palm of Yuichi's left hand was wrapped round and round in a bandage, and he had a bandage below his left eye and on the scruff of his neck.

"...I thought you were gonna die or something."

Sitting heavily on the bed, Yuichi explained the particulars of the accident. Since installing the fallen mirror was his first job, you reap what you sow, he grumbled.

"Well, good thing it didn't become a big deal. I'd be in a fix if the circle got banned from going there or something because of my injury."

"It's a problem for you, though. You look like you've really gotten into this lately."

"...Well, there're a lot of fresh and new things about it. At any rate, it's my first experience ever making things while learning from other people and cooperating with them."

"Making things?"

"If someone comes up with a new idea, we tackle it through discussion and adapt it to circumstances. For example, when making a display shelf, we decide where to position it, how the light hits the exhibit, and the color. It's like a culture festival every day."

Maybe because of his injury, Yuichi seemed a little drained. His speaking voice was soft, and a smile was just barely formed on the corners of his lips.

"But, oh well. I'll have to switch from the work I was heading up to something light that only requires one hand. It'll inconvenience everyone, and there's no way I'll still make that high hourly rate."

"You'll be fine if you try hard and recover. Asaka was praising you for being fast at working once you got the gist."

With an ardor that even he found mysterious, Wataru offered words of encouragement. It wasn't as if the loneliness he'd felt earlier had completely vanished, but he thought it would soon dissolve just from being with Yuichi this way.

That's pretty calculating for me, thought Wataru as he tried to come up with other ways to cheer Yuichi up.

"Oh, I know. Kazuki, aren't you're kind of inconvenienced with just one hand? Why don't I come by to make dinner for a while? For starters, tonight..."

"Thanks. But, I have no appetite."

"Does your injury hurt?"

It wasn't just an act of the imagination: Yuichi was feeling down, all right. The worried Wataru put both knees on the floor and peered up into Yuichi's face. He was relieved to hear that the injury would be fully healed in one week, so it wasn't that deep a cut, but maybe it was the shock that was powerful.

"Kazuki...?"

It was when Yuichi unexpectedly let slip a sigh that Wataru softly called his name.

"Wha!"

His wrist grabbed unexpectedly, Wataru was pulled in roughly. Unable to resist the sudden movement, he collapsed onto Yuichi's lap.

"Wh-What, all of a sudden?"

"There's something I want to ask you."

Sounding like he'd made up his mind, at that instant the confused Wataru braced his feelings. Unable to freely move his left hand, Wataru gazed back at Yuichi.

"What do you want to ask...?"

"A girl in the club told me. That you were there at work today. But instead of calling out to me, you practically ran for home."

"Well... "

"Also, when I got injured you were with Asaka. Am I wrong?"

"You're not wrong..."

This is terrible, Wataru murmured inside.

Yuichi found out he'd met with Masanobu in the worst possible way.

"I don't especially mind if you talk to him.

That's your free will, do as you see fit. But, wasn't the reason you came by to see me?"

"......"

Wataru couldn't answer right away.

Besides, however he tried to smooth this over, it could only sound like an excuse to Yuichi. Maybe if it'd be fine if it'd been someone else, but he'd been with Masanobu. He'd presumed upon Masanobu's kindness, even when he knew what feelings Yuichi held toward him. Of course he had to shoulder that risk.

"Wataru...say something..."

The pain in Yuichi's voice was saying "Offer me an excuse." So, Wataru tossed out the hesitation inside him, and decided to convey the words that honestly came to him.

"Kazuki... "

"Yeah?"

"Ever since the day we fought, I've been depressed. Until now, I've never felt pain due to your kindness. It was no wonder I was discouraged, wondering if something was wrong with me..."

"...And so?"

"So, I went to see you. I thought I'd face you, and knock out my anxiety. Because I couldn't find an answer alone, I wanted you to help me."

However, it was effectively what Masanobu said that helped him. Yuichi probably realized that. He waited without saying anything for Wataru to continue speaking.

"I thought, 'I really am weak.' I was conceited enough to think that when I came to your work, you'd probably be depressed, too. But you weren't. Work is work, and you were taking care of your responsibilities. I...even when I wanted that to be the case, it made me feel terribly lonely. It felt kind-of like you'd become someone I didn't know."

Above Yuichi's lap, his free right hand squeezed tightly into a fist. Miserable feelings and twisted thoughts blended, and Wataru wasn't able to look up.

"You said not to fake things...to tell you anything, but I really don't want to tell you something like this. I felt so lonely, though. I didn't want to see you laughing somewhere I wasn't at."

"And so you..."

Yuichi didn't finish the sentence.

He let out a heavy sigh and re-gripped Wataru's left hand.

"You're not even carrying the spare key, are you? Is that why you were waiting outside today?"

"Well...I was always with you when I came by here... Besides, I hadn't seen you since the fight, so the key's at home for..."

"One week."

Yuichi spat out, interrupting Wataru.

"Even though you haven't seen me in a week, you ignored me and chose Asaka. To top it off, your rationale was that you were lonely? You've gotta cut me a break here."

"Kazuki... "

"Do you remember what I said? You don't realize the look on your face when you talk to Asaka. That's why you can be alone with him so calmly."

"I...I don't understand what you're saying. The look on my face...? Why is it wrong for me to be alone with Asaka?"

"Good grief..."

His brow wrinkled, Yuichi hesitated for a short time. After the pause, peering into Wataru's eyes from close at hand, he clearly asserted:

"Don't depend on anyone but me."

"Eh... "

"That's the face you make, when you're with Asaka. What're you trying to get from him? What about me makes you feel insecure?"

"Insecure...about you...?"

Wataru forgot to even blink; he was so floored by what Yuichi had unexpectedly said. But before he could consider whether Yuichi was serious or not, his lips moved.

"I need...no one but you, Kazuki..."

That was the one solid thing. It was always Wataru's only truth.

"I've always only ever seen you. There've been painful times because of it, but I've never once regretted it. So, I haven't even had room to think about what face I make when I'm talking to Asaka."

"Wataru... "

"I always wonder what there is I can do when I'm with you. But, I don't see any answer, and sometimes it makes me very sad. But I can't tell you that...so..."

"......"

Yuichi kept quiet.

The complicated color that came to his eyes

conveyed that something was heavily wavering inside him.

"When I heard you'd gotten hurt...I worried and worried so much I couldn't stand it. It's true that I was with Asaka when it happened, but as I headed for the hospital I regretted it big-time. While I was absentmindedly drinking tea, what would've happened if it reached the point where I'd never see you again?"

"Don't kill me off in your head."

"But, if you'd stepped just a little differently it might've happened!"

"No it wouldn't'tve."

"You can say that because you don't know anything!"

"Huh...?"

Yuichi's face looked perplexed by Wataru's sudden outburst.

"What don't I know?"

"......"

"Hey. Say it, Wataru."

"That I..."

Even if it was by force of circumstance, Wataru spoke with extremely reluctant feelings.

"…love you...too much..."

"What?"

"That's what Asaka told me. It seemed like a pretty out-there thing to say, but it's no lie. I love you many times over. So, it doesn't matter at all what face I make in front of someone else."

While he was speaking frantically, the sensation from when he hurried to the hospital started to revive inside Wataru.

I don't care about the job or the trip. I want nothing more than be alone with you. While Wataru felt like his chest would burst with feelings, he earnestly pushed onward.

"True, Asaka has listened to a lot of my troubles. If you say that's me depending on him, then maybe so. But I wasn't able to tell you. I knew how much you cared about me. Because I thought it was wrong to have insecurity with no basis..."

"So that's it..."

Yuichi muttered with eyes of blank amazement.

The heavy air, which had been stifling until then, began to lift. Driven by strange feelings, Wataru quietly gazed once again at Yuichi's face.

"Kazuki...?"

"I..."

"......"

"Yeah, I really do hate Asaka."

"Kazuki... "

"Now I clearly see the reason why. His eyes rubbed me the wrong way."

"You don't have to say it like that..."

"Is there any other way to say it? I'm the only one you're allowed to depend on. And yet, he's able to snatch my privilege away like it's nothing. He's only two years older than me. It's too irrational to even be."

Yuichi really did seem vexed. He'd realized that the hazy grudge he'd held so long against Masanobu wasn't simply a case of likes repelling.

"...That's why I specifically asked you to come

by work. I wanted to tell him to his face to leave us alone. Those eyes of his that say he can do whatever he wants pissed me off from the start."

The look in his eyes was complicated. Wataru had wanted to push away those open arms that he could always retreat to. Yuichi had been made to taste his first sense of powerlessness at Masanobu's attitude like he could see through their dilemma.

"Kazuki..."

"I don't need some weird friend who pretends to understand. However people look at us, I love you, Wataru. It irritates me when I think of how that fails to get through to Asaka.

"......"

Wataru was deeply moved as he listened to Yuichi's confession. This was because Yuichi's "uprightness" that Masanobu commented on had completely seen through even these feelings.

"Kazuki... I love you..."

He didn't know what else to say. All emotions besides love had gone away somewhere.

Doubt, insecurity...the look in Masanobu's eyes, too.

"Wataru."

"I love you so much, Kazuki…"

"Wataru, don't cry."

"I...I'm not cryin'!"

"Silly...yes you are..."

Maybe Wataru's words had enchanted him, but the sound of bitterness disappeared bit by bit from Yuichi's voice.

As he slowly bent the upper half of his body downward, he licked just beside Wataru's eye.

"Sheesh. What are you, a kid?"

"What're you doing, all of a sudden...?"

"What do you mean, 'what'...?"

For an instant Yuichi was silent, like he'd been caught off-guard, and he gave a long, hard look back at Wataru. It was as if he'd totally forgotten he'd been grasping Wataru's left hand all this time.

Before long, Yuichi said in a voice full of conviction:

"I'm kissing you."

The next moment, a shadow once again fell over Wataru's eyes. Their lips met gently, and every complaint was sweetly shut away.

"Hn...!..."

Wataru's throat continuously purred. As if to soothe this, the bandaged left hand clumsily attached itself to his cheek.

Through open lips tongues made their way, entwined in a loquacious murmur. A deep sigh spilled from Wataru's lips, becoming the name of his beloved.

"Kazuki..."

He was filled to his fingertips.

With every kiss, Asaka's words became real feelings enveloping his body.

Wataru's body now knew that whatever doubts and insecurities arose, Yuichi's warmth tenderly dissolved them all.

"Ka...zuki..."

He quietly called out to him between kisses.

With each new kiss conferred as an answer, the movements of Yuichi's tongue whispered "I love you." to Wataru.

Irritated by his disabled left hand, Yuichi tried to draw Wataru up onto the bed. His heart packed full with a sweet premonition, Wataru himself moved to help him.

"...I love your voice."

Smiling thinly, Yuichi looked over at Wataru as he lay there. The soft radiance in his eyes communicated the sincere depth of his feelings more than any confession ever could.

"It's kind-of touching."

"Eh...?"

"It's been a really long time since I saw you from this angle. Hasn't it?"

Hearing these words from such a serious face made Wataru suddenly feel embarrassed. It was completely dark outside, but the lights in the apartment were on bright. The words and his gaze felt as if they would resound straight through his heart.

Yuichi leaned over and kissed him.

Lured by the movement of the mattress, Wataru, with his eyes closed, was reminded of a swaying spring sea.

Their blended sighs increased the sweetness, and before long Yuichi's kisses moved to his neck. The sensations Wataru had begun to forget could be felt quietly reawakening inside him.

"It's one consolation that it was my left hand that got injured."

As Yuichi exaggerated thusly, he playfully nudged at tender spots with the tip of his tongue. In the midst of the rising passion, Wataru realized he wanted him even more greedily than before.

"Your kisses... I really love those, Kazuki..."

"Just the kisses?"

"At times like these, I also love how your voice gets just a little softer. You usually sound so proud, but now it's a bit coquettish. Hey, Kazuki? When things are like this it feels like anything could happen and it'd be okay."

"How calculating of you."

While laughing, his sweet, proud voice fell upon Wataru's collarbone. Wataru closed his eyes again, and gave himself over to Yuichi's warmth.

The ever-present fragrance of his hair, the faint scent of a compress. Each time Yuichi kissed his skin, Wataru's chest became filled with pain. Embracing each other this way, focusing on each others' heartbeat, all at once the world seemed to be theirs.

As their lips were joined, articles of clothing fell to the floor in no particular order, and their bodies lay as bare as on the days they were born. Finding the act quite natural, this was how Wataru first knew his love for Yuichi.

"Kazuki, don't push yourself too hard. Your injury..."

"But it's what you want, isn't it?"

"Well, I..."

Turning red from the agitating line, Wataru brought his lips to meet the bandaged left hand. He remembered seeing how desperately Yuichi had fought with the mirror, and it pained his heart.

Leaving his left hand to Wataru, Yuichi gently stretched his right hand out to him.   The ardor the movements aroused soon materialized in a sigh from Wataru.

"Ka...zuki...!..."

"I love you, Wataru."

"Nn...!..."

Enduring aching pleasure, it took all Wataru had to nod. Even so, he knew for a certainty that beyond his closed eyelids Yuichi was smiling.

Overflowing feelings, and an over-feeling heart.

This sensation was indispensable to love, but at the same time it made it easy to lose sight of one's partner.

The graceful fingers wandering around Wataru's skin could easily produce pleasure, but sometimes they seemed like they might forget even so simple a result.

That's why I want us to make sure, time and again.

I want to make it known both with bodies and words.

"Kazuki... I love you..."

Wataru murmured in a shallow voice over his bared shoulder, prompting Yuichi to stop his lascivious fingers and answer "I love you, too" in Wataru's ear.

Body warmth melted them together, and heartbeats entwisted.

True affection, unfading however often they

embraced.

Yuichi's shoulder blade, covered by a hand, and the captivating sound of moist skin rubbing together here and there tenderly urged Wataru on.

While being rocked by the building wave, Wataru repeated "I love you" until he went hoarse.

"Kazuki sure is late..."

Wataru muttered into the silence, looking up at the rain cloud-filled sky. It was before the rainy season had truly started, and lately the weather had been less than stable every day.

"I may have needed an umbrella after all. I've been rained on plenty of times in this park."

A cluster of hydrangeas to his back, Wataru remembered this same season last year.

After he'd communicated his feelings, this was where he'd kissed Yuichi. Hidden in the vivid indigo shadows, they'd become intoxicated with happiness until they were dizzy.

Thus a year had passed, and now he waited once more for Yuichi in the same park. In his heart he kept a love deeper than before, and ties just a little stronger.

"Maybe I should try calling him..."

Today was Yuichi's birthday.

But it was already over ten minutes past their meeting time. It was rare for punctual Yuichi to be late without even calling. Some new problem... thought Wataru as he put himself on-guard, but just then an out-of-place cheerful voice called out.

"Sorry to keep you waiting, Wataru."

"H-Huh? Asaka?"

When he returned his gaze from the sky in high spirits, Wataru spoke in a drained, resigned voice. The person he thought was surely Yuichi was Masanobu.

Yuichi's job had ended last week, so it had been a while since Wataru had seen Masanobu's face. He stood there grinning, as always with his looks that drew their own looks from people , and his style reminiscent of a model.

"Asaka... Why're you here...?"

"Actually, I was just with Kazuki at the job site, and there was some unfinished work he wanted to wrap up no matter what. So, for the time being, I'm here to deliver the message and be a pinch hitter until he comes."

"The job site..."

"Yeah. His position lasted until last week, but you know how it goes... We're running a bit behind schedule, so he's helping us out. He's having an unexpected amount of fun with it, though. But, as always, he stubbornly refuses to join the circle. Maybe it's because he doesn't like me after all."

"No way..."

"But, here we are. Even though Kazuki said he'd call you on his cell and explain things. What, you hadn't heard anything?"

Wataru disconcertedly shook his head, but Masanobu didn't seem to be lying. However, for Yuichi to ask him of all people to come here seemed too unexpected to easily believe.

"But it's true, you know."

Masanobu said this while laughing, like the way Wataru lost his cool was much too funny to endure.

"Honestly, I was confused, too. But, I accepted it, thinking that being able to go on a date with you was a plus, even if it's as a stand-in. I said OK right away, and naturally he got a troubled look on his face. Too late for that now, I told him."

"They, he shouldn't have asked..."

"That's what I thought, too."

They looked at each other, and both burst into laughter. He sure didn't know what Yuichi's intention was, but Wataru too was happy to get to talk to Masanobu again this way.

"If Kazuki gave it the thumbs-up, it's okay with me too. What shall we do, then?"

"Let's see... On the way here, I kept thinking about this... If it's not a problem, I wonder if you'd listen to what I have to say for a bit."

"Huh...?"

"Wataru, you have entrance exams next year? Kazuki was saying how you probably won't have much time to see each other. I thought in that case, your chances to talk to me will be even rarer. Today might be the last one."

"I wouldn't say 'last'..."

Hearing it said formally like that, naturally it makes me feel a little lonely. It's like being told "We won't meet again" in a roundabout way.

"Uh, if you want to talk to me, please do so all you like. You've done nothing but encourage me this whole time."

"Thanks."

"I'm serious. You were a lot of help with what happened with Kazuki. So please, don't say sad things like 'this is the last time.'"

"Wataru… "

As Wataru drew close to enthusiasm, Masanobu got a slightly troubled look on his face. Wataru still didn't understand what the reason for this was.

But by the next instant, Masanobu had returned to his usual calm smile.

"Then, I'll take you up on that. Why don't we sit on that bench and talk?"

"Not a cafe or anything, you're sure?"

"Yeah. Actually, what I'm about to talk about may be a little stifling for you. So, I think it's better to be outside. As long as you don't mind, of course."

Even though what he said seemed to be weighty in nature, Masanobu's tone of voice was as cool as ever. Wataru gazed at the sky that looked like it would rain, and for Masanobu's sake requested silently Please let it hold out until we're done talking.

They sat next to each other on the bench, and Masanobu started talking like it was an everyday idle conversation.

"Wataru, I wonder if you remember. What I said about the girlfriend I used to have."

"I remember. Exceedingly cute and selfish. That's what you said."

"Yeah. I really thought about telling you this then... Actually, she passed away. Just about a year ago, in a traffic accident."

"Traffic accident... "

"Lots of things happened and we broke up, but even after that we remained friends. So, it was quite the shock for me."

"......"

I never thought the conversation would go like this. It had all gone so unexpectedly serious that Wataru didn't know what kind of expression he should wear.

But, there must be some meaning for him to expressly choose to tell me this. Thinking this, Wataru quietly inclined his ear.

"...I was dumped by her."

"What, you were? Are you kidding?"

Masanobu getting dumped was about as far from reality as Yuichi being in unrequited love. As if Wataru had suddenly seen through his heart, Masanobu quickly flashed a weak smile.

"It might sound arrogant, but at the time I thought that too. 'Are you kidding?' I'd wanted things to work out well with her, and I did everything I could for it to happen. But, I'm sure that must have worked against me."

"No way..."

"This is what she said."

Gazing quietly into Wataru's eyes, after an interval Masanobu's lips moved.

"That she loved me too much and it hurt."

"......"

"So, all I could do was break up with her. We still had feelings for each other, but we couldn't think of any other way at the time. I loved her for a long time, though. Thanks to that, I was pretty depressed after she died, so much that I was in danger of not passing that year. It's miserable, but I even had to drop a class..."

"That's how you got into Kazuki's class...?"

"Right. In that alone was I lucky."

Masanobu let out a long sigh and turned towards the dark sky. It didn't seem like Wataru's wish would be granted.

"Wataru. You understand, right? Why I chose to tell this personal story to you?"

"Yes."

"You and she are very similar. Not the way you look, but your attitude towards love. That's why I said I can't leave you be. When I first saw you with Kazuki in the cafe, I felt very...anxious."

"......"

"You were gazing at Kazuki a bit proudly. You were absorbed, and very happy. I was nailed to the spot by you. You had the same eyes she did when she'd look at me."

"Then, that time... "

Wataru finally came to understand.

Masanobu's direct, transparent stare...it was the mysterious look that made Wataru's heart confused and brought about both unease and relief. That was definitely not a coincidence.

"Wataru, you were terribly confused. But I was quite confused inside, too. I knew I had to see you again, no matter what."

"Wh-Why?"

"Because I didn't want you destroying yourself with your own love like she did."

It sounded like he could have been talking to himself, but Masanobu answered in a resolute tone.

"I was aware that it might have been untimely interference. But the reality that Kazuki and I were the same type spurred my feelings on. You two looked like you were going to hurt each other. But, Kazuki had warned me and it wasn't a good situation for personal conversation. So, I dragged him into the part-time job."

"Eh... "

"You see, I thought if the situation allowed it, you would show up at his work. And it happened just as I thought. Otherwise, I'd have no point of contact with you, especially with you still being a high schooler."

"Why did you go that far...?"

"I told you. I couldn't leave you be. I used to be just like Kazuki is now. She loved me desperately, but by the end she was completely exhausted. "I want to go back to being friends," she cried. I didn't want the same thing to happen to you and Kazuki."

"......"

"You two really overdid it at the job. You had to push aside the dilemma of not being able to openly act as lovers in front of everyone, and deal with the disorientation of a changing environment. So, to stir things up a little I tried speaking meanly to Kazuki. When I did, his reaction was so much more acute than I expected, it surprised me."

But, smiled Masanobu. As if he'd remembered something, his voice became cheerful.

"What surprised me even more was you, Wataru. I never thought you would yell at him. At that point, I looked at you with completely different eyes. You're the type who derives strength when they're in a corner."

"But, that was because Kazuki..."

"You've got to fight, didn't you say?"

Masanobu sighed as if to say "I give up."

"You usually seemed to be lacking in the courage department, so it seemed like an irregularity to me. But, your expression is what made me realize everything. The reason Kazuki chose you, even though you're a boy. I'm sure he was unconsciously searching for someone who'd become strong in loving him."

"Become...strong..."

"That's also what I wanted from her. So, I understand. You're tough like a weed, and optimistic like the sun...also delicate like the ring on your finger. The reason Kazuki is engrossed with you is probably because he found all those things within you."

Once he'd finished saying that, the first drop hit Masanobu's shoulder. He looked up at the crying sky, and his eyes went somewhere far away.

I really like him, Wataru thought sincerely.

A face thinking of someone with all its might. That's not something that only Masanobu's dead ex-girlfriend and I have. The profile he's showing me is no doubt thinking of how precious someone is.

That's right, nodded Wataru.

The day Yuichi had his accident, we shared a bed as we embraced. That warmth was everything about love. We didn't need anything else.

"Asaka, thanks."

"Eh?"

"Until now I've been filled with feelings of love for Kazuki, but I get the feeling I've gotten the hang a little more of being loved unreservedly."

"Wataru... "

"I feel confident now. Even if the locale changes, even if there's less time we can spend together, I'm sure Kazuki won't change. Because I can believe that like me, he's absorbed in this."

Besides, Wataru added internally.

If even then my feelings get too strong, when my emotions get stubborn, I'll remember Masanobu. I'll use the "good at relaxing" skill I learned from him in my love for Yuichi.

Perhaps his monologue reached Masanobu, for he nodded slightly.

"It's about time for Kazuki to show up."

After Masanobu stared tenderly at the sky that had started to rain, he slowly presented his left hand to Wataru while still sitting on the bench.

It was a hand filled to the fingertips with affection.

"Farewell, Wataru."

"Eh..."

"It's a lonesome word, but there's no other way to say it. But, this 'farewell' doesn't mean 'never again.' I really like you a lot. So, think of it as a pause until we meet again."

"Asaka... "

"I don't suppose you'll forget me. Naturally, I

won't forget you either. Do you see? Now, a 'connection' has been formed between us even without Kazuki. That's why I told you what I did."

Masanobu's words were just like music. Wataru was intoxicated with the pleasantness, but at the same time it was painful, like his chest was being constricted.

As he went to take the hand in front of him, Wataru unconsciously extended his own left hand. The ring of restored silver shone, and the loving finger touched Masanobu.

"Farewell."

Sensing that it was the most appropriate word for this setting, Wataru imitated him as he spoke.

The rain was coming down slowly, but they departed from that place seeking shelter. As they walked along not saying much, there was Yuichi leaning against the park gate.

"You done with work, Kazuki?"

Wataru ran up to him in bounding steps, and Yuichi casually held an umbrella over him. Masanobu came up afterwards, and the two simply nodded at each other.

"Kazuki...?"

"Sorry to keep you waiting. I asked Masanobu to contact me if the two of you moved, but I never thought you two'd be walking through the rain. Talk about eccentric."

"You know, you don't have to talk like..."

"Isn't it you who's the eccentric one?"

Masanobu spoke with a smile, interrupting Wataru. Without flinching, Yuichi shifted his gaze to look Masanobu square in the eye.

"Thanks for pinch hitting."

"No, it's my pleasure. Thanks to that, I was able to enjoy talking with Wataru. Hey, Kazuki?"

"Yes?"

"Is this all right? Could it have been some kind of peace offering to me?"

His searching gaze was definitely not smiling as much as his mouth. Wataru alone inclined his head, not understanding what this was about, and Yuichi, who until then had a sour look on his face, suddenly returned a smile to Masanobu.

"I don't see you as an enemy."

"......"

Masanobu fell silent for an instant, as if he felt ashamed.

Before long, he burst out laughing a little, said "Okay, see you," and walked away.

"What was all that, Kazuki?"

Wataru muttered like he was offended as he watched Masanobu running away through the rain.

"You started talking about enemies and whatever nonsense. Asaka is an extremely good person. Don't say such rude things to him."

"......"

"Okay?"

"...Okay."

Once more, Yuichi smiled.

Plap-plap, the raindrops struck the umbrella. Yuichi deftly retook the umbrella from Wataru, said "Shall we go, too?" and walked off.

"Kazuki... "

Wataru opened his mouth, and his voice was engulfed in the sound of the rain.

"Happy birthday."

"Thanks. But you know, it's one problem after the next every year. The time in particular it looks like it's going to run long, so we'd better be careful."

"What problem?"

Wataru was alarmed for a moment that there was still something. But Yuichi just looked at him with deep meaning and didn't say anything.

"Ah, right. More importantly, I hope you remember? Why I worked so hard at that job in the first place. It was all so we could go on a trip."

"Yeah, of course I know that."

"Then I'm guessing you got permission from your parents a long time ago?"

Saying this, what Yuichi pulled out of his jacket breast pocket were two envelopes sporting blue airline logos on white backgrounds.

"That's... "

"You took forever deciding where we'd go, so I decided myself. We at least had to go where there's ocean. So ocean it is. And by the week after next we'll be in Okinawa. All right?"

"O-Okinawa?"

"Nice, huh? Just once, I wanted to try eating those blue fish. Wataru, by the week after next we'll be on the beach in Okinawa. Four days and three nights, our first trip. Get ready for it."

"Y...Yeah."

Starting to nod reflexively, Wataru was caught by Yuichi saying "Get ready for it."

As a baffled look took over his face, Yuichi sent a mean glance his way.

"Speaking of which...where's my present?"

"Huh?!"

"Today is my birthday. Didn't you just wish me happy birthday?"

"Ugh… "

"So, what about the present?"

Even though he knew the answer, Yuichi was enjoying watching Wataru's troubled face.

Just the other day he had refused to receive a present from someone who couldn't even manage to get money together for the trip, and now he was acting like this, just as Wataru was taking him seriously.

When Wataru was at a loss for an answer, Yuichi finally burst into laughter. It was a voice of happiness that refused to lose to the sound of the rain.

"So, like I said. Get ready for it. I'm going to throw my weight around as much as possible in Okinawa. At any rate, I'm the sponsor. Work hard, Wataru. You'll do whatever I say, right?"

"Kazuki!"

"Looks like it's going to be a fun trip."

Next to his good-humored lover, the miserable Wataru felt like a little servant.

Well, maybe that's more proof that I've loved, and I might be pretty naive for thinking it.

As Wataru smiled ruefully, Yuichi gently brought his lips in closer under the shielding umbrella.

The seasons seemed about to change again.
The anniversary kiss held an aroma of rain.

Eternity of the Palm

"Wow...is it hot here...!"

The moment he stepped outside Naha Airport, the warm wind wrapped around his whole body. Wataru Fujii inhaled very deeply, and tried stretching his arms and legs, stiff from the cramped plane, as far as he could.

"I wonder what the temperature is here? It's only 1PM, so it might get even hotter."

"Probably. According to the announcement on the plane, it'll go up to 30° Celsius."

"30°...seriously?!"

Wataru looked dumbfounded by the calm comment from Yuichi Kazuki, his boyfriend. It was still right in the middle of the rainy season in Tokyo, so the light sprinkle at Haneda Airport had made it a little chilly. However, the sunlight where they landed pierced his skin with warmth, and every time the wind blew, their noses were tickled with the thick, sweet fragrance of grass. The long-forgotten sense of summer was vividly revived, and Wataru knew he'd gotten a head-start on the season.

"Man, what a huge deal to come to the south."

"You're exaggerating. That was, at best, a two-and-a half-hour flight."

"'At best...you know, you're not excited enough!"

"Oh, yeah?"

A discouraged Wataru scowled at him, but Yuichi remained composed to the point of obnoxiousness. However, it was obvious at a glance that his good-humored eyes weren't as cold as his voice. He probably doesn't want to be seen as defenselessly happy. He's trying too hard, Wataru thought to himself, but he cleverly pretended not to notice.

The rainy season had just ended in Okinawa in late June; there was a forecast for consecutive days of nice weather. This was also their first vacation experience together. It was probably impossible to tell Wataru not to be in high spirits. He cheerfully repositioned his nylon travel bag, and bounded after Yuichi, who had wordlessly started walking.

"You know, though, that was a really pretty airport. There was a huge fish tank in the entry hall, and a pretty girl in native dress standing there. I was impressed, like 'So, this is Okinawa.'"

"They opened a monorail this year, so that's extremely convenient. I'm pretty sure the airport used to be smaller and plainer, too. Places here and there have been changing since the Okinawa Summit."

"Wow...you know a lot about it, Kazuki. Is this not your first time here?"

"Yeah, did I not tell you? Diving's been my brother's hobby since his college days. I've been here several times for that."

"Your brother...oh, Takako's father. Didn't you say he was an architect...?"

"Right. But he's busy now, and it doesn't look like he has any time for diving."

When Yuichi nodded, a cheerful voice suddenly called out, "Mitsuboshi is this way!" When they looked, a young man was excitedly waving his hand next to a van stopped on the road shoulder. A rental company's gaudy logo was painted on the white exterior, and at a glance they knew it was for guest reception. Wataru tried to ignore it, thinking That's got nothing to do with us, but surprisingly, Yuichi wasted no time in heading straight to it.

"H-Hey, Kazuki! That's not a taxi."

"Dummy, of course I can tell that. Just hurry up and follow me."

"Ehh?!"

Ignoring of the perplexed Wataru, Yuichi informed the man of his name. Wataru quickly followed and seated himself in the van.

Inside was a group of what looked like three college girls, but when Yuichi became visible they suddenly stopped talking. Again...?, Wataru sighed to himself, but of course he couldn't let it get to him every single time. When it came to Yuichi's attractive face and figure, there was no stopping his garnering attention, be it good or bad, and after dating him for a year, Wataru had gotten somewhat used to the stares. He was only relieved for a moment, however, as one of the girls spoke up in an overly-familiar voice, as if she's just been waiting for him to sit down next to Yuichi.

"Hey, hey! You two were both on that plane, weren't you?"

"Huh...?"

"I mean, you really stood out. So, are you on a

trip together?"

"Th-that's correct..."

"Wow. Two boys together?"

"......"

"Isn't that a little odd?"

She was probably bantering on in an effort to flirt, but it made Wataru's expression stiffen. Whatever the reasons, there was no helping the fact that two guys on a trip together looked a bit strange. Even coming this far didn't change the discomfort of their social position. As Wataru unconsciously started to sigh over this, Yuichi spoke up in a blunt tone.

"Sorry, but could you leave us be? He and I both have one already."

"Have one? One what...?"

Unable to catch the meaning of his sudden words, the girls had baffled looks on their faces. Yuichi quickly softened his eyes, and with a fearless expression on his face slowly put his left hand up to near his cheek.

On the long elegant ring finger was a silver ring with a thin gold line in the center.

"Is...that..."

"As you can see, it's a promise ring. My sweetheart is a very jealous person, and it's bad news if I take it off."

"B-But, you're not together right now. We can at least talk..."

"Unfortunately, I don't care to when I'm wearing this."

"Are you serious? Is he the same way?"

Maybe because Yuichi had talked about his love life so directly, the girls looked half-amazed. Wataru hurriedly nodded, and they were completely subdued; they stopped trying to strike up a conversation.

"We apologize for the wait. Now we'll be off!"

The driver smiled and the van slowly started moving. Wataru lowered his voice and whispered to Yuichi, who strained to listen as if nothing had happened.

"Since when were you wearing your ring? I could've sworn on the plane..."

"We've come all the way to Okinawa, I can't be worried about other people looking at us."

Then, I should've worn mine too... It's safe in my wallet."

"Your wallet? It's not a lucky money charm, you know."

With a delighted looking smile, Yuichi pushed his hair up with his left hand. The ring shining on his finger was the same design as the one sparkling in Wataru's wallet. They each, in their own way, safely kept the ring that had brought them together. Lots of things had happened, and they had come to refrain from wearing them during everyday life as a whole, but seeing one back on their partner's finger always warmed their hearts.

"I swear... Who's the jealous sweetheart...?"

"You say something?"

"Not especially. It's nothing."

Responding curtly to hide his embarrassment, Wataru gazed happily at Yuichi's ring finger.

I've got to hurry and put my ring on too once we reach the hotel. As if he could hear that internal monologue, Yuichi smiled beautifully in profile.

Now I get it..., Wataru realized keenly.

This was why Yuichi told him to bring some of his favorite CDs.

"Since when the heck did you..."

"Hn? You say something?"

"So...Kazuki, since when have you had your license?!"

Wataru glared from the passenger seat at Yuichi, who gripped the steering wheel with a triumphant look on his face. A pleasant bossa-nova melody had been drifting from the CD player installed in the car, and it was one of Yuichi's favorite discs. Listening to the light singing voice for the summer sun, Wataru pouted his lips in frustration.

"You know, if the disc was meant for driving, you should have told me in the first place. I thought for sure they were for listening to at the hotel or something, so all I brought were ones good for putting someone to sleep."

"Ah, that's why it's such a quiet lineup!"

"Well yeah, I thought they'd be nice and mellow for playing in the room. By my way of thinking at least..."

"What, is that what you've been sulking about?"

The teasing tone of Yuichi's voice made Wataru look away sullenly.

"...I'm saying you held out on me!"

"About what?"

"What do you mean, 'what'? You've never once said a word about being able to drive..."

"It's not like I was hiding it. Besides, I got my license before I started seeing you. I started taking lessons just after becoming a senior, and by my birthday I'd gotten my provisional. You know, our school didn't prohibit acquiring a license if you use it to commute."

Yuichi's explanation flowed smoothly, almost as if he had anticipated Wataru's reaction. But Wataru still had feelings of dissatisfaction. When Yuichi started college, he'd taken the opportunity to start living on his own, and as their chances to spend time together at his apartment had increased recently, Wataru thought he had come to understand a lot more about his lover: music he liked, and his taste in movies. The pace at which he bought clothes, the kinds of seasonings he liked, and so on and so forth. One by one, these small things were becoming familiar with them. After all that, overlooking something this basic was a little strange.

"'Before you started seeing me' sounds kind-of iffy."

"To put it another way, it was just before we met."

"Well…that's true."

"I never dreamed that the first one outside family I'd give a ride to would be you."

"......"

With that one deeply emotional sentiment, Wataru's sour look suddenly became uncertain. Yuichi stole a sidelong glance, and his calm expression and

elegant way of handling the steering wheel were cool enough to fall in love with all over again. The rental car was a small local model, but by just settling in his seat he could see several degrees higher. Maybe it's the bias of love, Wataru smiled ruefully inside, but stares came their way simultaneously from heads turning in cars stopped on either side of them at a traffic light, and they couldn't all have been that dizzy.

Wataru put his left elbow on the window frame, turned to Yuichi's demure face, and spoke.

"I've kind of got a weird feeling about this. I'd meant to already be mostly used to you as a college student. But I never imagined you driving like this back when you were in a uniform."

"No one at the college knows either. First off, I don't have a car, so there's no chance to show it."

"Then I really am the only one you've given a ride to. Maybe I'll forgive you for keeping it quiet."

"How kind of you."

Yuichi smiled with the cheerful murmur. Outside, unfamiliar building after building of square stone passed by outside the window, telling Wataru that this was definitely his first time here.

Right now, he was alone with Yuichi in an unfamiliar place.

Sitting next to his lover, Wataru became uncertain about how he had lived up until the point of meeting Yuichi. That's how special this love was. Feelings of discomfort in the face of the fact that they were both men were unavoidable, but he knew such things were trivial when confronted with his emotions.

It's the same for him in the driver's seat, but I wonder how many other sides of him I'll discover on this trip. With this simple thought, Wataru's heart swelled with anticipation.

"Why'd you stop talking all of a sudden?"

"Eh..."

"If you're worried about something, speak up."

With these words, Yuichi's left hand pushed lightly on Wataru's temple. Not discerning the sweet sentimentality, Wataru hurriedly smoothed over his expression.

"It's fine, I'm not worried about anything. My parents gave their permission for the trip quicker than I expected, and since the school establishment anniversary comes after the weekend and it's a three-day weekend, I managed to just miss one other day. Kawamura said he'd loan me his notes to cover for it..."

"Even if you don't borrow from him, I'll take a look. If you'll be a day behind, I'll get you back on track quickly."

"Well, my parents went for this because you've taken such good care of me. It looks like they trust you all the way. Besides, they think I'm staying with one of your relatives, so they're not worried. Though thanks to that, I have to bring them a souvenir!"

"Good thing I have a cell phone. There's no way we could have told them the hotel phone number. But..."

His face went a little still, and for a moment Yuichi hesitated. Then the left hand that had pushed before brushed Wataru's hair gently, and Yuichi lowered his tone a little as he said, "I'm sorry."

"I made you lie to your parents…"

"Come on... I told you to knock off the guardian attitude."

"Wataru..."

"I'm here with you because I love you. We're not really doing anything bad, and the ends justify the means. Man, you really are an honor student down deep, Kazuki. There's nothing to worry about."

He spoke roughly on purpose, but even Wataru was happy for Yuichi's concern. He held the hand that had brushed his hair in his and slowly moved it away, smiling and saying lightly, "But, thanks."

Turned towards the unexpectedly smiling face, Yuichi seemed to be quite flustered. He quickly drew his left hand back, seemed to intentionally clear his throat, and adopted a stiff expression. He had once confessed that he was "charmed by Wataru's smile," and even now this seemed to be what he was most susceptible to.

Eventually the car entered the open freeway, and Yuichi increased their speed a bit. They were probably headed towards the hotel, but Wataru still hadn't been told where they were staying. Yuichi was the sponsor of this trip, so arrangements and agenda were all left up to him, but "You'll see when we get there" was all the answer he could get out of him. Wataru had asked what in the world he was up to, half out of interest and half out of anticipation, but whatever place he was led to, he decided he'd truly enjoy it.

At any rate, it's my last break before exams.

As they plunged forward into the deep blue sky,

their four days were about to begin.

After a forty-minute drive, the car finally arrived at the hotel's front entrance. The smiling staff greeted them, and their uniform light short-sleeve white shirts really did make it seem like a southern hotel.

"K...Kazuki?"

"Hm?"

"Is this...where we're going to stay?"

"That's right. What are you gaping at?"

Leaving the car key with the staff, Yuichi got out first and walked towards the lobby. Wataru, however, was enchanted by the unreal spectacle unfolding before his eyes, and didn't move for a time.

From the spacious vestibule to the terrace in back overlooking the ocean, absolutely nothing obstructed the wind. Because of this, despite being surrounded by high ceilings and thick trim, it was a space made to feel open and fresh. On a refined bamboo sofa set found in many Asian resorts, a newly-arrived guest was holding a delivered drink in one hand and elegantly going through the check-in process. Yuichi, too, sat at a nearby sofa with an air of familiarity, and soon began talking in a frank way to a man in a suit who seemed to be a manager.

"So then, you two desire a twin for three nights. As you wished, we have prepared a room with an ocean view. Our staff member on-duty will now escort you there."

"Thank you. We appreciate it."

"There was also a phone call from your brother.

He seems to be as busy as always."

"Yes, he's always on business trips. I haven't seen him lately."

"I see. If at all possible, I'd have enjoyed hearing his latest travel stories."

"I'll let him know. I'll also mention how the service has been further refined, and how it's even cozier."

Standing to the side and listening to their conversation, Wataru realized that Yuichi was already familiar with this extravagant resort hotel, and it surprised him a second time. He was totally into the idea of their first trip, but any way he looked at it this didn't seem to be a hotel on-par with what a mere high school student could afford. Despite that, Yuichi had brought him here like it was a matter of course. Maybe it was indeed a good thing to rely upon his good graces?

"Kazuki...uh..."

"What is it? Come on, here comes the elevator."

Paying Wataru's hardened face no mind, Yuichi was warmly greeting the staff member carrying their luggage. His brisk mood, regardless of who he dealt with, and his charming, calm demeanor were why he was looked up to as the best student in high school. It was sometimes odd that they were only a year apart.

It's kind of...aggravating how well it suits him...this kind of place...

Then, I wonder what the people in the hotel think about his companion, who's looked bewildered this whole time? When he though that, all of a sudden

Wataru's heart felt heavy.

I knew I should have paid for at least a little myself.

Yuichi had resolutely forbidden Wataru, as an exam student, to get a job, so he didn't have much money of his own to use. Wataru had told himself it was "just this once," but he hadn't intended on this high a level of luxury and he honestly felt sorry.

But, if we were at some inn or a business hotel on the outskirts, Kazuki probably would've been horribly anxious...

No matter how much his family was involved in dentistry, there was no way Yuichi was extremely rich. However, his refined style, which was often mistaken for that of a model, as well as his refined bearing created the overall impression that he wouldn't lose out, no matter how magnificent a setting he stood up against.

Compared to someone this unique, Wataru was "ordinary" to the bitter end.

His appearance was by no means shabby, but he grew hazy all at once standing next to Yuichi's outstanding form. His partner was so well-made, he couldn't even summon the willpower to get depressed. Wataru always thought about wanting to become at least a man who wouldn't seem out-of-place with Yuichi.

Right...for example, like Asaka...

Suddenly, Masanobu Asaka's handsome face came to Wataru's mind. As Yuichi's upperclassman, Masanobu was a young man blessed with various talents that were no less impressive than the seemingly one-of-a-kind Yuichi. The sight of the two of them together where Yuichi used to work was beautifully balanced, just like a painting.

But if I told that to Kazuki, he'd probably make a horrible face!

Actually, Wataru liked even his angry looks quite a bit. Fundamentally well-mannered Yuichi didn't really let negative feelings come to the surface openly. For whatever reason, Masanobu was the only person he'd openly show wariness towards, and Wataru thought it was somewhat "cute." Of course, he had no idea what maliciousness would befall him if that were found out, so he hadn't said anything about it.

"Hey, Wataru. What've you been spacing-out about?"

"Huh?"

"We're at the room. Here's your luggage."

Sometime while Wataru had been lost in thought, the staff member had left. He was being peered at searchingly by Yuichi, and he hurriedly averted his eyes.

"Whoa...that's so pretty... "

The next instant, he spoke without thinking. A cream soda-colored ocean had jumped into his full field of vision. Wataru ran to the open terrace, and his eyes lit up like a child's.

"You can see the ocean from the terrace! It's deep blue, like a jewel..."

"We'll go check it out later. It's the hotel's private beach, so it's clean and uncrowded."

"Private beach..."

"Wataru?"

"......"

Yuichi dubiously addressed Wataru, who had fallen silent again.

"You've been acting weird. Do you dislike the hotel?"

"No...no, it's not that..."

"Then, why...?"

"I was thinking it was, like, beyond our means."

"Huh?"

Maybe he hadn't been expecting Wataru's remark, but for an instant Yuichi's face looked like he'd been caught off-guard. But, as if he's reorganized his feelings, he soon spoke to his lover calmly. "What do you mean?"

"I just wanted to prepare the most pleasant place I could think of for you."

"Yeah...I know that very well. I mean, this really is a nice hotel. I don't just mean high-class; it's not putting on airs like some midtown hotel. The people here are nice and good-natured, and wind comes through all the building, so it feels really great. I'm so happy that you thought to bring me here."

"Then..."

"But, isn't the burden all on you in the end? I really don't think we could have stayed at a hotel like this if I'd covered my half. That bothers me. I mean, wasn't this originally supposed to be our trip to celebrate your birthday? If that's true, I should have done the inviting..."

"Wataru... "

Bringing this up at such a late date probably only made things harder for Yuichi. Even though he knew that, Wataru couldn't keep quiet. It was very painful to accept Yuichi's kindness. It was too irritating for him in his current position as an exam student with so many restrictions.

"I still have no way of bringing you to a hotel like this, Kazuki. You know, for a while here I'm not going to be able to do anything but study for entrance exams. So...I..."

"Gotcha."

Yuichi let out a large sigh while Wataru was still talking. When Wataru succumbed to insecurity and lowered his head, Yuichi was suddenly right before him with his arms crossed.

Yuichi stood there and stared, and in the next moment he made his eyes glitter teasingly. Wataru, not understanding, looked on blankly, then the corners of Yuichi's lips raised pleasantly.

"I must confess, the hotel fee was practically free."

"Practically free...?"

"Right. You heard my conversation with the hotel manager? My big brother's involved with the plans for this place. To be exact, an architectural unit centered around him does the work."

"Architectural unit..."

Hearing the term for the first time, Wataru's face became more and more baffled. But he at least knew well what Yuichi was getting at. The point was that one of his relatives was involved with this building, so it probably meant they could stay there for a discounted room rate. Put that way, Wataru understood.

"Geez... Wouldn't someone usually be openly glad to be invited by someone else to a hotel this nice? Instead, I get 'beyond our means.'"

"Sorry!"

"I had a feeling you'd say that, though."

Yuichi softly embraced Wataru, his head hanging, with both hands. Wataru submitted himself calmly, and Yuichi divulged light laughter and stiffened his arms.

"You told me you can't do anything."

"Yeah..."

"Don't forget what I told you before. Didn't I say I'd take care of you until your exams are over? Thankfully, I don't need to push myself that much right now, so just relax and depend on me. Your having fun is what will make me the most happy."

"Kazuki... "

Yuichi gently pushed Wataru, at a loss for an answer, away and gazed at him again. His prior cheerfulness was gone, and his look had a boundlessly feverish tinge. I wonder if there's anyone who could maintain reason with those eyes bearing down so close, thought Wataru seriously.

"Hey, Wataru..."

"Eh?"

"Promise me. Even in the middle of the night or at dawn, even if it's just for five minutes I don't care. From now on, desire to see me whenever you can. Only miss me when we can't see each other."

"......"

"I said the same thing a little while ago, didn't I? To me, your desire has far more value than a trip with a first-class hotel and a car. So, this time at least, let me indulge until I'm satisfied. All right?"

All right, Wataru nodded before he even thought too much. At the same time, he realized that all the inferiority and indebtedness and everything he'd felt had been foreseen by Yuichi.

Wataru was happier than anything to comply with Yuichi's request. Well, then, he considered. He would enjoy the lifestyle gap from the heart without being nervous about luxury beyond their means. He would treat these experiences as preparation for the day when he would be a man on par with his "esteemed" boyfriend who was always several steps ahead of him.

Until that day arrived, he'd stop sighing to himself.

"Yeah...okay, I hear you."

Wataru regained the determined light in his eyes, and brought his lips closer to Yuichi's.

"But, I take no responsibility for regrets later on. I'm talking willfulness without limit."

"Talk on. First time's free, the second costs you a kiss."

"There're conditions attached?"

The mutter mixed with a rueful smile was cut off by a sweet sensation. Soft lips overlapped, and Wataru gently caught Yuichi's fever through his tongue. Each time he was kissed deeply and shallowly, his heart ached. He had a feeling he'd never be healed of this intense pain, no matter how many thousands of kisses they exchanged.

Tongue tips probing teasingly, a sigh spilling over made their lips moist. Wataru stirred as if troubled, and Yuichi's arms firmly pulled him closer. His head now embraced, Wataru's lips were snatched away hotly. The backs of his eyelids glittering with a surprising intensity, Wataru unconsciously and ferociously grasped Yuichi's shirt.

"Wow..."

Having disengaged his lips, Yuichi said in a bewildered voice:

"And here I thought we'd go out once we put our stuff away."

"You were just saying we should go to the beach."

"That I did...so, what now?"

The inviting tone of voice fell captivatingly on Wataru's ears. Accompanied by a smile, the words were filled with an undeniable charm. At any rate, there was no way he could go out in public with a disarmed expression like this.

"So what now, Wataru?"

"You truly are evil..."

When Wataru made up his mind and lightly shifted his weight, Yuichi, still holding him, collapsed onto the bed behind them, as if he's predicted this. The high-quality mattress sank softly, and the two laughed lightly at the same time.

Like a design, their summer clothes had been

removed and strewn across the floor.

Yuichi, his top half bare, suddenly stopped moving his fingers through Wataru's T-shirt, got up once from the bed, and quietly closed the window connected to the terrace. At that moment, the sound of a wave had grown strong, and now the inside of the room fell as silent as the bottom of the sea. Wataru slowly raised his upper half and spread his arms to welcome Yuichi back.

"That was a surprise. Talk about service."

"It's your birthday celebration, just two weeks late."

He exaggerated, but somewhere there was a lingering awkwardness from acts he wasn't used to, although, after several times, resistance while being with Yuichi was largely gone. Wataru was always the first one to be played with for the sake of pleasure, and sometimes, he wanted to be the one to give first. He'd been secretly harboring that aspiration for this trip.

"Kazuki...thank you."

His love overflowed just from his naked skin being touched. When Wataru looked up at Yuichi's face, he said with as natural a smile as possible:

"Thank you for what?"

"Yeah. Actually, when talk of the trip first came up, I had thought I really wanted to go to the beach. So, when I heard you'd chosen Okinawa, I was a little surprised. And I was happy that you somehow picked up on it."

"Okay... Lately the peanut gallery's been annoying, and things have been seeming more and more cramped, so I wanted to try being in an open landscape once, to get rid of all the excess noise."

"By 'peanut gallery,' you mean Asaka?"

"There is that. But...it has other meanings. As was expected, I can't do things the same way as when I was in high school. I want to keep important things in mind, like the future, and you..."

"But, I'm in love with you."

When Wataru said it like a whisper, Yuichi opened his eyes as if surprised. The tone of his voice was full of hope, and wasn't mixed with a bit of anxiety.

"No matter how annoying it is around us, you look directly at me, Kazuki. I learned that from your college job and meeting Asaka, so I came to be comforted by watching you back. As our circumstances steadily change, there'd be no end to the drama if I got more insecure. But, I'm sure we'll be fine. Because no matter what happens, I...love you."

"...You cheeky monkey."

His voice had some sadness mixed into it. After a long kiss, Yuichi's loving gaze fell on Wataru, and he ruffled his hair. Wataru, without thinking, frowned, and was kissed lightly on both his eyelids and temples as if he was being pacified.

"The more we do this, the less I want to leave the room."

"After being on a plane two-and-a-half hours to see the ocean?"

"It's your fault, Wataru. You're the one who got all cute on me."

"C-Cute...?"

"Right. It's even better when you're sullen."

Just when a person's trying to make a serious confession. Wataru started to get mad, but Yuichi seemed to have finally regained his own pace. Wearing an unyielding smile, he lightly touched Wataru's collarbone with his fingertips.

"Wataru... I love you..."

In the abruptly rousing atmosphere, Wataru failed to find a response and turned red. His hard-fought determination now gone, his pulse doubled all of a sudden at Yuichi's sweet voice and the movements of his fingertips. Thanks to the blood rushing to his head, it became very difficult to focus on pleasing his partner. He was aggravated with Yuichi and his composed smile, like he could sense Wataru's state of mind.

"I love you, Wataru. I really am happy I'm able to be on this trip with you."

"D...Don't say it like you're trying to woo me..."

"I can't help that. I am indeed trying to woo you."

While sweetly biting his earlobe, Yuichi spoke in a thrillingly romantic voice. Wataru reflexively stiffened his body, but his lips were accustomed enough to this to patiently melt that away. Each time Yuichi moved his kisses bit by bit from earlobe to neck, then to left and right collarbones, a light giddiness attacked Wataru. In the afternoon sun-filled room, only the sense of rubbing skin and the timbre of kisses stretched out just like an ephemeral ripple.

"Ka...zuki... "

Half-awake and half-asleep, Wataru struggled

against a state of only being loved. But his hands feebly wandered through the air, and before he knew it he was clinging firmly to Yuichi's shoulder blade. The stirred-up, slight fever soon became a blaze, and before his now-stuttering voice could finish calling out a word, it continued to desire Yuichi. The feelings of pleasure scattered here and there gradually melted into one and changed into the form of a great ache inside Wataru.

"Hn...!..."

"Wataru? Wataru, are you okay...?"

"Eh...?"

"You're kind-of, more than usual..."

For some reason, Yuichi was unusually concerned. The scent of his favorite shampoo stood out faintly from his flushed skin, and Wataru blinked his sweaty eyes several times.

"Uh...something wrong...?"

"Well, I...I thought you had passed out or something..."

"Kazuki... "

"Hm?"

He tried to somehow reign in his hard breathing, but there was so much heat in his excited voice. However, Yuichi was looking at him like he was worried, so Wataru stopped hesitating and decided to just say it.

"The reason I spaced out was, well...because it felt like I was being taken somewhere. So...that's why..."

"......"

"I, I'm saying...don't stop."

Mustering up meager courage to say it, he ended

up so embarrassed that he glared up at him. Yuichi opened his eyes for an instant, but he soon nodded kindly, like he had stifled a laugh.

The lightness of the pecking caresses expressed Yuichi's enlivened heart. While thinking Maybe a request like that one falls under willfulness, Wataru endured his own bashfulness and closed his eyes. Before long, he was washed away by an immense wave of pleasure, and thereafter was inexplicably rushed up to an elevated place. Each time he sweetly raised his voice, new passion burst into life from the depths of his body.

Hugged tightly by Yuichi and unable to escape, Wataru was consumed to the limit. His sense of time and place gone somewhere far away; all that remained were their heartbeats and warmth. Wataru continued to call out to Yuichi as if delirious, his whole body made to shudder as Yuichi's long breath that passed over his ears.

"I love you, Wataru."

Yuichi didn't stop loving Wataru the way he wanted to until Wataru's body sunk into the bed from fatigue. His lips visited every spot he could see, and he trifled with him in a loving manner many times over. Sometimes intensely, sometimes affectionately, it was like accepting words as confessions many times more serious than face value.

"Kazuki...I love you... "

Maybe this is what they mean by "the only two people in the world."

Wataru, engulfed in happiness, sunk deeper into his vague consciousness.

We spent nearly all the first day of our precious trip in bed.

Those were the first words that came to Wataru's mind once he awoke from a mud-like sleep.

"No wonder my whole body's sluggish..."

The room was a twin, but they'd attached the two semi-double beds, so Yuichi was sleeping right next to him. Wataru muttered dimly, and he was surprised to hear a cheerful "Did you say something?" answer him from the direction of the terrace.

"Looks like nice weather again today. It could possibly get hotter than yesterday."

"Tough, aren't you... Kazuki, you're already up?"

"Of course. It's way past eight already. How about breakfast? Want to go get some?"

Standing beside the bed, Yuichi had a refreshed expression, like he'd already taken a shower. Of course you'd be energetic...thought Wataru bitterly, then suddenly their faces were close together and he was being stared at with a serious look.

"Wh-What, all of a sudden...? You startled me."

"Well...are you feeling okay? Should we get room service like we did last night?"

"Room service?"

"I'm saying I don't mind if we eat here in the room."

"I-I'm fine! Wait a minute, I'll hurry and grab a shower!"

When he hurriedly jumped off the bed and

glanced back over his shoulder, Yuichi was smiling happily. Last night, they'd had no energy to go out for food so they'd settled for dinner from room service, but wondering whether there were any signs of their love affair lingering in the room, Wataru ran out to the terrace while the hotel staff prepared the food cart. Yuichi played it cool, and not worrying whether the sheets were messed up on only one bed, he smiled smoothly as he signed the bill.

"Breakfast is until ten. You can take your time."

The teasing voice followed Wataru into the bathroom. Inside was a broad bathtub and a separate glass-doored shower booth, and the tiled floor was still a little wet. What kinds of things was Yuichi really thinking about, standing here while I was asleep? I wonder if he could remember a sweeter, more rousing time since we've been together.

"I don't think I could forget it, either..."

When he removed the robe that had been provided and looked casually in the mirror, several red marks stood out here and there below his left collarbone and on his side. Even though he's usually careful not to leave anything behind, it looks like last night Yuichi got really into it. I don't mind, though. I'm happy. But...

"So much for going into the water..."

Emitting a luxurious sigh, Wataru smiled wryly as he twisted the shower faucet.

Ordering breakfast from the four-star restaurant in the hotel was a matter of choosing your own place to suit your tastes. Both Wataru and Yuichi were hungry, so they decided on an all-you-can-eat buffet style cafe. It was the most ideal, with open-terrace seating, and they could enjoy breakfast while feeling the pleasant sea breeze. They headed for the table they were directed to, hurried to finish off breakfast, and saw far-off people relaxing on the beach.

"Nice... Today's ideal weather for swimming in the ocean."

"Like I said, I'm sorry."

"It's pretty hot, but I can't even wear a well-ventilated shirt!"

"Okay, I get it. What do you want to eat, Wataru? I'll go get it for you."

Wataru had complained terribly after his shower, so naturally Yuichi must have felt awkward. A rarity for him, he was in a humble mood. I wonder how long it'll last... Wataru fought down the urge to burst out laughing, and was just about to open his mouth to say "Let's see..."

"Oh? Is that you, Wataru?"

"Huh?"

"Ahh, I knew it. And Kazuki's with you, too."

Impossible, Wataru reflexively doubted his ears. At the same time, he saw the look in Yuichi's eyes sharpen. Seeing this, Wataru's own intuition was unexpectedly proven correct. Yes, he didn't know anyone else who would call out his name in that soft a tone.

But, if the owner of the voice was "him," he couldn't figure out why he'd be there.

"Asaka..."

There he stood, with those cool looks that stood out all the more in a crowded place, and a warm smile that naturally made you want to trust him. Wataru unconsciously got up from his chair and stared in blank amazement as Masanobu approached.

"Wh-Why are you here? Are you on a trip, too?"

"Yeah, well...something of that nature... You two're on one...right?"

"That's right... Uh, Kazuki's birthday was this month, and so..."

"Ahh, okay. Kazuki, you worked hard at that job."

Holding his tray in both hands, Masanobu answered with his unchanging, kind eyes, and when he looked at Yuichi, who was overtly trying to avoid his gaze, the expression in Yuichi's eyes crumbled even further.

"As for me, I always wanted to see the old residential architecture left over in Okinawa. I took advantage of the fact that someone I know happened to be coming here for business."

"In Okinawa...?"

"That's right. But, I never expected to meet up with you guys here."

"Are you really surprised?"

"K-Kazuki!"

Wataru tried to hurriedly follow up on Yuichi's curtly muttered words. But Masanobu laughed cheerfully and said "Sorry to intrude on your breakfast," like he'd paid it no mind at all.

"I plan to be here two or three more days, but what about you guys?"

"We just arrived yesterday, and we'll return to Tokyo the day after tomorrow."

"Okay. Then, there's still time. If you'd like, we could have dinner together tonight..."

"Asaka. Isn't it a bad idea to ignore your acquaintance?"

Yuichi spoke up again, in an obviously annoyed manner. He didn't notice at all when the troubled Wataru gave him a reproachful look. But sure enough, without losing even a fragment of his expression Masanobu remained calm to the end and said, "Sorry, Wataru. Maybe that was a little forward?"

"I was so happy to see you after all this time. I got a carried away... But, you two would rather be alone. And unfortunately, Kazuki doesn't much like me."

"No, it's not really that..."

"Wataru."

"I'm sorry. Um, our schedule is quite packed...so meal dates are a bit difficult..."

Wataru definitely didn't hate Masanobu. In fact, it could be said that he held good will towards him. But naturally, he didn't have the courage to go against Yuichi's stern voice, and it was the truth that they wanted to spend the trip by themselves. Though it felt inexcusable, Masanobu nodded slightly and readily consented.

"You don't need to worry about it. This is your first time in Okinawa, isn't it? Then, you two enjoy..."

"Thank you for your consideration. Come on, let's hurry and get food."

Before Wataru could answer, Yuichi bluntly ended the conversation. He stood up in displeasure, grabbed Wataru's left arm roughly, and pulled him along, looking unsmilingly at Masanobu.

"If you're excuse us, Asaka."

"E-Excuse us."

Continuously dragged along, Wataru bowed his head with all his might. While smiling a significant smile, Masanobu watched them leave like he was enjoying himself.

"Listen, Kazuki. Whatever the case, there's no call for that attitude."

Wataru protested reservedly while they crossed the 170-meter steel bridge that continued on to an underwater observatory. Since they couldn't go in the water, they had decided to first see the facilities at the hotel site. Built from a promontory, you could apparently go down a spiral staircase and enjoy what it's like four meters underwater through glass. However, Yuichi's encounter with Masanobu seemed to have been so unamusing that he maintained a sour look no matter what Wataru said.

"He's just an upperclassman in your circle..."

"For the record, I don't remember ever joining his circle. I just helped out."

"Then there's no need to be sullen with me."

"Yeah? Then I should just be happy that you got to see him again?"

Wataru sighed in exasperation at the uncharacteristic, childish remark. It wasn't that he didn't understand why Yuichi would be in a bad mood after abruptly encountering someone he didn't get along with on their trip. But, if he kept up that wrinkled brow the whole time, the ocean and blue sky they'd come to see would be ruined.

"Why does it have to be this way where Asaka is concerned? It's a little weird, Kazuki. Of course, as you're so similar to him, there may be some side of his you don't like, but Asaka is quite...hey, are you listening?"

"...Fish."

"Heh?"

Just when Wataru thought he had stopped suddenly, Yuichi put both hands on the handrail and leaned far forward. Several meters down, the ocean spread out in a shining azure color, glittering where the sunlight struck. Attracted by the enthusiastic profile, Wataru peered with him at the water's surface, and a swarm of vividly colored fish swam into view. Aquariums aside, this was the first time he'd ever seen this many fish in a natural environment. All at once, he forgot everything, and his mouth opened excitedly.

"Wow, they're so deep blue. Oh, that one's yellow. Are those called anemone fish?"

"Look. There's a school of porcupine fish over there."

"No way, really? I've never seen any alive before! Which reminds me, aren't those blue ones swimming over there the ones you said you wanted to eat, Kazuki?"

"Those're probably blue devil damsels. The ones I was talking about are bigger...but you've got a good memory if you remember that. Actually, my brother is totally bad with fish. After coming all the way to Okinawa, we couldn't go to one seafood place. But, they might actually be good..."

"Then tonight let's take the challenge. Wasn't there a restaurant called Seafood Market or something on the way here? I'm not particular, so let's go."

"......"

"Kazuki...?"

Before Wataru realized it, Yuichi's gaze had shifted from the fish to him. As Wataru met his gaze defenselessly, he knew that Yuichi's feelings had changed in an instant from merry to tense.

"What..."

"Sorry, Wataru."

The brusque utterance overflowed from Yuichi's lips. Indifferent of Wataru's surprise at the unforeseen words, he suddenly looked back at the sea and sighed in an unpleasant way.

"I'm the one who decided to go to the seaside and get rid of all the annoyances. I can't go laying into you and breaking the vow the day after we get here."

"You had vowed...?"

"Secretly."

Theatrically putting his right hand over his heart, Yuichi purposefully made a meek face. Wataru felt inspired to place his own left hand over Yuichi's, and with his eyes fixed on his ring which he hadn't worn in a while, declared, "Then, I'll make a secret vow, too."

"Vow? What're you vowing?"

"To be your servant for the rest of the trip. I'll carry it out properly."

"Servant? Oh, that. That makes me happy, but it's not 'secret' at all."

"I was honestly thinking of forgetting about it. It seemed like it would be a bad idea to consent to it. But, you being so docile feels kind of weird."

"Give me a break..."

Sullenly shaking off Wataru's hand, Yuichi started walking quickly like he was mad. While following behind him, Wataru hurriedly called out, "Hey, Kazuki. Wait up!"

"What, are you mad? Come on, Kazuki..."

Once again, Yuichi's footsteps slowly stopped.

As Wataru adopted a defensive posture, Yuichi turned around, smiling boldly with his characteristically intense look.

"You forgot to say 'master,' Wataru."

After they'd had their fill of southern fish between the underwater observatory and a glass-bottomed boat, they decided to go into town for lunch. Yuichi drove them north of the hotel, and they entered a place reputed to have good Okinawa soba noodles. It was a small shop that couldn't hold more than ten people, but according to Yuichi this place was the best.

"Kazuki... Okinawa soba's the only thing on the menu..."

"Not like you should really mind. We came here to eat that."

Looking strangely at Wataru, who was in mute amazement, Yuichi ordered two sobas from the lady working there. The inside of the shop was already starting to get busy, but the lady courteously answered "Oh, long time no see." and flashed a friendly smile.

"How many years has it been? Your brother's not with you? You know, that handsome one."

"I apologize for that, but today I have a special friend along with me."

"Oh, isn't he a cute boy! Well, maybe we'll have to make him a VIP from now on."

Cracking a joke and disappearing into the back, Wataru for some reason felt tickled by her. Maybe it was because the shop's appearance stirred up nostalgia for the neighborhood ramen shop he used to frequent when he was little. It was old, small, and lacking affectation, but the warmth of the people working there gradually got through to him.

"Despite how it looks, it's quite famous."

Yuichi offered this explanation upon reading Wataru's expression.

"It's an old place, established ninety years ago, and fans come from all over the country to eat here."

"Ahh, so that's why the walls are covered with colored paper. But, places like this have their charm."

"My brother's a favorite of the lady who works here, so I'm happy she remembers me when it's been years since I've shown my face. At any rate, the last time I was here was before Takako was born."

"Then, you came here a lot until then. You must get along well with your brother."

Until now it hadn't been a very intense conversation, so Wataru felt somehow happy. However, after Yuichi hesitated briefly, he said, "Get along well, eh..."

"We're far apart in age, so of course I got affection from him. When I think about it, maybe the way I saw him was something close to admiration. After he was a student, he wandered from place to place overseas. Once in a while he'd come home, and take me out diving or something. Our parents were extremely worried about that type of behavior, but through my young eyes...it was pretty cool."

"Wow..."

"Even if there was something I couldn't tell them, I could discuss things with him. Of course, occasionally one of us would get upset and pick a fight...but he was hardly ever around."

The soba arrived just then, so the conversation cut off. But for Yuichi to say that much, Wataru took more than a little interest in what kind of person his brother must be. He certainly had never dreamed he would hear the word "admiration" come from Yuichi's mouth. Even though Yuichi himself got nothing but looks of admiration and envy from everyone around him, it meant there was more to his world than Wataru realized.

"Ahh, this is good. It really is!"

Wataru tried his first mouthful of soba while still thinking, but his lively voice unthinkingly spoke up. In his first challenge of Okinawa soba, the soup was a weak color but the stock came through well enough. From there, Wataru gleefully brought the noodles up to his mouth, and for a while devoted himself entirely to eating.

"Huh? What's the matter, Kazuki? Your soba's getting stale."

"Eh..."

"What gives? You haven't eaten any of it yet."

When he suddenly paid attention again, Yuichi's bowl was still untouched. Wataru, who'd been engrossed in eating, looked back and forth between Yuichi and his soba with slightly subdued feelings.

"You were the one recommending how good this place was. Or are you feeling bad?"

"No...sorry, it's nothing. I was just thinking about something."

"Don't tell me you're still thinking about Asaka..."

"No, stupid, not that."

Quickly picking up his chopsticks, Yuichi decidedly denied it.

"...He was saying earlier. He's here with an acquaintance."

"Yeah."

"I was a little stuck on that. Never mind, don't worry about it."

"......"

Even if he was told not to worry, he couldn't just be fine after seeing that vaguely depressed face. But he also didn't want to waste the good mood they'd worked hard to have going with overly invasive questions, so Wataru kept quiet. Maybe it was because Yuichi felt the same way that he forced himself to smile.

But, just like when they watched the fish before, that smile soon became a real one. Yuichi slurped a mouthful of soba, said "Sure enough, good stuff," became completely enthused, and finally regained his usual cheerfulness.

Asaka's acquaintance... I wonder if Kazuki knows who it is...

A faint doubt crossed Wataru's heart. He couldn't even guess, but if it was enough for Yuichi to be concerned about, it might have been someone problematic. If he asked about it now he probably wouldn't get an answer, and if it went badly it would only spoil the mood of the trip. Rather than say something careless, he picked up his bowl in both hands and drained the remaining soup in one gulp.

"Ahh, that was tasty..."

"What do we do now? It's still early afternoon. Even though we can't go in the water, want to go to the beach since we're here? I can lead you to plenty of nice spots."

Yuichi turned the key while Wataru sighed satisfyingly in the passenger seat. He wore sunglasses because of the glare when driving, but as he sat there waiting for an answer he looked kind-of like an incognito celebrity out having a good time.

"The beach...you're right, I'd really like to go..."

"Then, that decides it. Let's drive a bit and head

for a nearby island. While we're at it, we should visit the Okinawa Churaumi Aquarium that opened recently. The truth is the water is prettier if you go to an outlying island not connected by a bridge, but you can only see so many places your first time here."

"First time...oh. You mean this isn't the last time..."

"Of course it isn't!"

Yuichi declared this casually. He believed in the future like it was a matter of course, not even doubting that Wataru would be beside him from now on. This way of talking made Wataru a bit happy, and his expression slackened naturally.

Unlike yesterday, what flowed from the speakers was Latin pop with a nice tempo. The CD that Yuichi had bought just for the cover was awesome background music for flying down the coast. Wataru gazed out the window in a pleasant mood, and he wanted to laugh out-loud at what it must mean when he was the "servant" yet he had someone to be his own escort, driver, or whatever.

"What are you grinning about? It's creepy."

"Nothing. I was just thinking how happy I am."

"Huh?"

"At the least, during these four days I might be the happiest exam student in the world."

"Hmm..."

Maybe he was taken aback by the honest thought, but the sharp comeback he'd seemed to have prepared never came. Thinking this unusual, Wataru tried stealing a glance at his profile, but he couldn't read anything from eyes hidden by the sunglasses. About the time he disappointedly sank into his seat, their car gently came to a stop to wait for a light. At that exact moment, Yuichi deftly undid his seat belt and brought his face in close.

Before there was time to think their lips were joined, and by the time Wataru came around Yuichi was back in his original spot. As proof that it wasn't a dream, two elementary school boys halfway through the intersection were staring amazedly in their direction. Black knapsacks on their backs, they looked alternatingly at Wataru and Yuichi as if frantically confirming that they were both male. But as the light soon changed to green, they ran off before their looks at Wataru turned to glares.

"Kazukiii..."

"What?   A servant has to fight through shyness."

"D-Didn't I tell you before to cut that out in front of children...?!"

"Oh, you mean Takako?   You don't need to worry about it so much. First of all, I think by the time she grows up couples like us will have more civil rights."

"That's not the issue..."

Halfway attacked by exhaustion, Wataru gave up on his sermon.

Maybe because he had once managed to kiss Wataru in front of his niece as a rough way of getting her to stop crying about marrying him, Yuichi had a rather defiant attitude regarding kissing.

Please don't let them seeing two men kissing be a bad influence on the future of those boys. That was the one grace Wataru prayed for.

As would be expected from how many times Yuichi had visited Okinawa, every place he took Wataru held almost nothing but new wonders and excitement for him.

The beach he took him to was on a small island over a bridge from the main island, and a coral reef stretched all the way from the shoals out to open sea. There were lots of people moving about with inner tubes, even where it looked shallow enough for them to stand on the bottom. But even that was dangerous, said Yuichi with a frown. Apparently, it was common for people to come away with lacerated limbs as a result of inadvertently scraping against the coral.

"However, if you go walking, there are also ridiculously huge sea slugs scattered around the sea floor."

"Ugh...I don't want to step on one...!"

"You think? It really gives you goose bumps for a second..."

Yuichi was excessively serious while staring at the water, as if maybe he'd experienced it himself. It didn't make Wataru shiver just imagining the sensation of stepping on one, but it was somewhat funny to hear it talked about so grimly.

After deciding to definitely go into the water tomorrow, they next went to Churaumi Aquarium, the home of the world's largest water tank. Thanks to it being the weekend it was terribly crowded, but here Wataru was nailed to the spot by the sight of leisurely swimming giant manta rays and whale sharks, and it felt rather impossible to return to the world of reality.

That was understandable, though. In any case, their field of vision was dominated by a huge tank on the scale of 7500 tons. Wataru was teased afterwards by Yuichi that he looked just like a kindergartner, gazing at the migratory fish with their hungry eyes.

"You know, isn't there any other way to say it? You were overwhelmed too, weren't you?"

"Of course, naturally it's intense. But I wasn't standing there slack-jawed like a certain someone I know."

"Y...You have any proof?!"

Sitting opposite each other in the aquarium cafeteria, they were seriously discussing such foolish things. Yuichi triumphantly held out his cell, on the face of which was a picture taken of Wataru "slack-jawed."

They made their way back to the hotel, absorbing themselves in stops along the way, browsing through a souvenir shop and studying a Ryukyu glass artisan's studio. For dinner they placed a reservation by-phone at Seafood Market that Wataru had talked about at the underwater observatory. The place had just opened this year, and you could have the fish of your choice cooked however you liked it.

"It's based on Thai cooking, so there might be a lot of spicy food. Are you okay with that?"

"That's fine. I love spicy. Now you can finally

have your way too, Kazuki."

"...As for me, I wouldn't mind if it wasn't so affected a place. In Naha, there's a famous public market, and on the second floor dining hall they cook the ingredients you buy from the fish market.

"Okay. Should we go there, then?"

"No...it's all right."

"Hm?"

When then came back to the room to take showers, Yuichi had strangely adopted a downcast attitude and it shocked Wataru a bit. While they'd hung out at the beach and aquarium it had seemed like he'd totally forgotten it, but now Yuichi had returned to the depressed expression he'd had earlier in the day.

I knew it, something must be up... But it doesn't look like he's going to tell me anything if I ask.

With the blue fish he wanted to eat right before his eyes, why was he acting so deflated? Letting Yuichi have the first shower, Wataru sunk onto the sofa while he thought over various things.

Could he be worried about running into Asaka again...?

Any way you looked at it, coincidences shouldn't be able to happen that often. Sure, the restaurant was one of the hotel's tenants, but this area was dotted with more places to eat than you could shake a stick at. And first and foremost, Yuichi wasn't the type of man to mope over such a thing...much less would he change his own plans because of Masanobu.

In that case...what could it be...?

Just then, Yuichi's cell, which had been left on

the table, started ringing. Wataru stared at it with a start, and tried calling out, "Kazuki, your cell's ringing." But, his words must have been concealed by the sound of the water, since no response came from the bathroom. It looked like there was nothing to do but take it to him.

"...Uh?"

When he reached out to the still-ringing cell, he unthinkingly opened his eyes wide. Caller IDs came up on the front on Yuichi's model of cell, and the characters flashing there were what caught his attention.

"Is this...?"

The mystery of where Yuichi's mind had been all day came together naturally after seeing the caller's name.

The name that came up on the LCD was "Shohei Kazuki."

"Mr. Kazuki, reservation for two? This way, please."

When they passed through the elegant door of the restaurant, a staff member dressed in a neat-looking white uniform met them courteously. Taking advantage of being built on a coastland location, the sound of waves was especially noticeable from the open terrace they were led to. The faint lighting that emphasized the darkness and the quivering flame of the lamp on the table, coupled with the sea breeze, produced a romantic southern sea evening. This place usually would have been much too classy for Wataru to feel totally at-ease, except that it was a resort area, so the comfortable atmosphere and large number of patrons in light clothing allowed Wataru to relax.

But, he was only relieved for a moment.

On the menus they were given were specified hors d'oeuvres, soups, meat dishes, fish dishes, the ingredients of each, and several different methods of cooking. As Yuichi had said, different kinds of seafood were prepared on a counter covered in ice, and patrons could select what they wanted to eat from there. However, Wataru went white when he saw that any one course on the menu was the price of a full course most other places.

"Kazuki...hey, Kazuki..."

"What, why're you pale?"

Trying to hide behind his menu as he spoke, Yuichi, who had until now looked depressed, was taken aback as he looked at Wataru. Maybe what had been on his mind the whole time was how to pay for this place? It would be terrible if something innocent he said earlier that day had resulted in making a reservation at a restaurant a bit beyond their means. His mind made up, Wataru began speaking resolutely.

"Let's just cancel and go somewhere else!"

"Huh? What's this about, all of a sudden?"

"This place is absurdly expensive. If it's blue fish you want, can't we eat those at the market you talked about? Let's give up on this for tonight..."

"Look, calm down. You sure are acting odd."

Yuichi tried to smooth over his disturbed feelings, but maybe he perceived that Wataru was serious, because he put his menu down on the table. Then he said, "Come on, let's start by looking at the fish."

Thinking that would make it harder to leave, Wataru frantically shook his head, but Yuichi had no intention of listening as he walked towards the counter, as if to urge Wataru on. Black tiger shrimp, crabs of various sizes, scallops, and whatnot were alive in tanks, but the fish were neatly displayed, almost as if someone had painted brilliant colors on top of the ice.

"Those are some big fish... Maybe I'll have each half seasoned differently."

"Is this any time to talk like that? I plan to pay for my share, but even so I can't handle treating you, too."

"Treat...what the heck are you talking about?"

"Sorry, Kazuki. Maybe if it was the ¥600 soba we had at lunch..."

"...Wataru."

"Wh-What?"

"Are you dense?"

The insult "dense" had flown from his lips so easily that, for a moment, Wataru was speechless. Finally, Yuichi's expression lightened, and he laughed lightly, as if to say he couldn't help how funny it was.

"Geez...so that's what you were thinking. You want pale and said 'Let's leave,' so you had me wondering what was up."

"B-But wait, don't tell me a high-class place like this..."

"Didn't I tell you? The hotel bill's practically free. With our budget, we can eat somewhat extravagantly without it breaking the bank. That's why I got the part-time job."

Yuichi was still laughing as he said this. Apparently Wataru was needlessly anxious over the meal cost. But in that case, what had been darkening Yuichi's face earlier?

Wataru thought about asking, but Yuichi had already started talking to a staff member wearing kitchen clothes about cooking while pointing to various fish. Not wanting to rehash it now that Yuichi's mood was finally improved, Wataru decided to give up on pursuing the mystery.

On the staff's recommendation, Yuichi decided to sauté half of the blue fish called iwabuchi he'd chosen, and steam the other half with soy sauce. Wataru thought that alone was plenty, but Yuichi had hit his stride, and he started steadily adding food until eventually, in addition to two fish dishes, tom yam kung full of salmon slices, butter fried scallops, and a special salad with Goya dressing were brought to them one after the next.

"This is...kind-of nuts..."

The many dishes lined up in front of Wataru were overwhelming. The thick sweet-and-sour sauce spread on the fish astonished him, the way the good flavor of the scallops spread throughout the mouth as soon as they were bitten into moved him, and before he knew it he'd downed his meal in a daze.

Yuichi was gazing at Wataru in a satisfied way; it was like seeing Wataru's joyous face made him happier than eating his own food. At times, Wataru would sense the gaze and look up, and the way Yuichi would make himself look sullen to hide his embarrassment was proof more than anything.

"Hahh, it almost feels like we did nothing but eat today. It sure was good, though..."

"The fruit is yet to come. You all right?"

"Fine, fine. You know how the fruit's on-display by itself away from the fish counter? I only just looked over there for the first time myself. So, I look forward to what you ordered from it."

"Then, I'd like to tell you something while we eat."

"Tell? Like what?"

Wataru asked back, not thinking very deeply since was off his guard from being so full. Maybe that made it all the easier to say, as Yuichi took a breath and totally changed the mood as his face became serious.

"Actually..."

"Yeah?"

"My brother's coming here in a bit."

"Uh..."

"Shohei Kazuki. You know that cell phone call earlier? I called him back while you were in the shower. And he told me he was here on business at our hotel."

"Uhh?!"

Just as Wataru started to get out of his seat, the fruit arrived, as if it had been timed. It was cut bite-size and served in Ryukyu glass, making it seem just like toy gems.

"Thank you for waiting. A combination platter of papaya, apple mango, cherry, starfruit, passion fruit, pineapple, and island bananas. Please apply sweet champagne to suit your taste."

"Hey, now that's extravagant. Looks like I came

at a good time."

A peaceful voice rung out behind the female staff member who was offering the explanation. When Wataru, still not fully recovered from the shock, sluggishly looked in its direction, it was Masanobu who had unexpectedly appeared.

"Good evening, Wataru. And Kazuki."

"Oh, Asaka..."

"You're too early."

Yuichi sighed very deeply, and displayed a truly annoyed bearing. The staff member showed tact in bowing and quickly walking away, and Masanobu smiled once again.

"Did you two have your fill of Okinawa today?"

"H...Hello... Uh, are you...?"

"Eh? Did Kazuki not tell you? We were going to meet here after dinner."

"Uh, but, that's..."

Kazuki's brother and... As he tried to complete that thought, suddenly what Yuichi said earlier in the day came to Wataru's mind. During lunch, in the middle of eating soba, he'd said "I'm stuck on Asaka's acquaintance."

"Ah. So then, is your acquaintance...?"

"Yup, that's right. See, he's walking towards the table now."

Masanobu looked away to direct attention. Wataru followed the direction he was looking. There, even in the subdued lighting, was a man in a suit who distinctly stood out.

"Is that...?"

Just from that, Wataru forgot what he was talking about like he was bewitched.

He had heard that Yuichi's brother was close to a dozen years older than them, but any way you looked at the man coming towards them, he couldn't be beyond his mid-20s. It definitely wasn't because he had a boyish face, but because something like an atmosphere emitted from his entire body, making him full of youthful energy.

The light style of his high quality linen suit lacked the smack of incompleteness of Yuichi or Masanobu, and it made his whole body ooze with a refined adult presence. What didn't give him a flippant impression, despite his apparent youthfulness, was probably the content radiance in his eyes.

"Is that...Kazuki's...?"

So, this is what dazzling one's eyes means, thought Wataru. In looks Yuichi definitely compared favorably with his brother, but no one else could imitate this overpowering sense of presence.

His skin appeared flawless, but the arrangement of his features brought even more out of his face, in a good way. He flawlessly made his own expression, full of self-confidence, which stopped just short of the line of arrogance. The entire time he directly approached their table, Wataru couldn't take his eyes off the charming smile playing out on his lips. That was the strength of the aura his whole body boasted of.

"Are you finished with work, Shohei?"

"More or less. I caught dinner on the way here.

This place only does fish, after all."

"You really do dislike seafood. A man definitely is not to be judged by his appearance."

"Don't be silly. That's what makes it interesting."

Shohei cheerfully addressed Masanobu's joke, then finally looked at Wataru and Yuichi. It might have been pure imagination, but he seemed to subtly adjust his own impression as he stood before them. The suffocating sense of oppression vanished, and a face transformed into a friendly "Yuichi's brother" face appeared. Because he had been so intense before, he didn't speak right away.

"Why're you in Okinawa?"

Yuichi spoke sharply, with upturned eyes, taking the initiative. It was like the seed of the bad mood that had been smoldering since morning sprouted all at once. His sullen tone and severe look had fallen several degrees below even his usual self. However, whatever Shohei was thinking, he appeared to ignore Yuichi as if he'd never spoken and instead suddenly peered at Wataru's face. The scent of men's cologne swept over the tip of his nose, and it made Wataru more nervous.

"...You're the one."

Shohei muttered shortly and grinned at Wataru.

"You must be Takako's former fiancé. Your name was..."

"F-Fujii. My name is Wataru Fujii."

"Yeah, that was it. Fujii. Pleased to meet you, I'm Yuichi's brother Shohei."

He said without giving the others time to butt in,

and extended his right hand.

With sweet-scented fruit between them, the four men faced each other at the table. The three of them possessed crowd-catching looks, and Wataru felt like he'd become the only commoner.

No, a commoner wouldn't be so bad. I'm a servant right now, a servant...

Despite chiding himself with self-derision, he didn't even have the willpower to laugh. Flooded with obvious attention from the surrounding tables, Masanobu was the first to open his mouth.

"May I have some of this?"

"...Suit yourself."

"Ah, then please use this, Asaka."

In place of the unsociable Yuichi, Wataru timidly passed his fork over. Masanobu accepted it with a smile and a "Thank you," and encouraged Wataru to eat it with him. In all honesty he had long since lost his appetite, but he couldn't bear to not be eating now. While thinking from the bottom of his heart how glad he was that Masanobu was here, Wataru partook slowly of the fruit.

While shooting a sidelong glance at this, Yuichi opened his mouth in a mix of a sigh and the following:

"When did you plan a business trip to Okinawa? When I told you over the phone about my trip, you didn't say a word about it. In fact, even Mr. Suzuyama the hotel manager didn't know anything..."

"That's because I arrived late last night. This meeting could have been held in Tokyo, but in any case I needed to fly to the actual location. I figured if I was going anyway, I might as well see my little brother after so long. You haven't come by our place lately; it's made Takako lonely."

"Coming all the way to Okinawa just to..."

Not finishing his sentence, Yuichi turned away from his brother suddenly. His unusually childish attitude reinforced for Wataru that the two of them were brothers. From his own perspective Yuichi seemed older and adult-like, with a faultless composure no matter what happened, but seeing him facing his older brother like this fully filled Wataru with the sense that he was still only nineteen, and still in the process of growing.

"Hey, Wataru. If you don't mind, I'd like to pour champagne on the rest."

"Eh...ah, sure."

"I actually usually like to drink it, but well, this isn't the atmosphere for a toast."

Perhaps guessing at Wataru's anxiety, Masanobu engaged him in conversation about this and that. After watching their exchange, Shohei brought his gaze slowly back to Yuichi.

"It's rare for you not to look someone in the eye while talking to them."

"......"

"Well, maybe it's understandable, a relative showing up when you probably were trying to kick your heels up."

"Don't smile and say that, it ticks me off."

Shohei warded off even the words of resistance with his impassive face. As he couldn't bear to be the only one looking the other way, Wataru made up his mind and addressed Shohei.

"Um, you can have some fruit too if you'd like, Shohei."

"Thanks Fujii. Sorry to wedge myself in here so suddenly."

"Y...You didn't really..."

"I've heard about you from Masanobu, as well. You're a senior this year? That's no picnic."

"Yes, well..."

It may have been because he felt timid, but all he could do was give a vague response. He had faced Yuichi's relatives plenty of times, starting with Toko, but he was out of his element when it came to Shohei. It might have been because he still didn't clearly understand the reason he had shown up in front of them.

"You don't need to be so tense. Shohei is a good guy."

Masanobu lowered his voice softly and whispered in Wataru's ear. But Wataru honestly had some doubt deep down even towards Masanobu. This morning, when they met him in the café, he really did make it seem like it was a coincidence, but what was actually going on? Shohei's manner seemed to suggest that he thought he'd run into Yuichi on his business trip, and in that case it wouldn't be strange for Masanobu to have been aware of it, too.

Asaka doesn't seem like the kind of person to do this for kicks, though...

Masanobu had acknowledged before that Wataru and Yuichi were lovers. So he knew that the nuance of this trip was a bit different from two friends going together. Even so, there had to be some reason for him to show up along with Yuichi's brother.

But then, why did he keep quiet about it this morning...?

At this point, Wataru could truly understand why Yuichi had been absent-minded. If he had been thinking that Asaka's "acquaintance" could be his brother, no wonder he had trouble enjoying the trip.

And it was especially strange if the brother in question was someone this compelling and unique...

"Then since you offered, I'll have a little."

Shohei's vigorous voice yanked Wataru back to reality. He hurriedly raised his head and squarely met the grinning Shohei's eyes. In quite a normal manner he asked Wataru, "Could you pass me a fork, too?"

"Ah, yes...here."

Wataru quickly took a spare fork out of the rattan basket placed near him. While courteously accepting it, Shohei murmured:

"Is that ring you're wearing the one you got back from Takako?"

"Eh?"

"Your left hand. I was thinking a boy like you is a rare type."

For an instant he regretfully thought Oh crap, but it was too late. At some point Shohei's line of sight had settled on Wataru's left hand defenselessly sitting on the table. When Wataru earnestly attempted to smooth his expression over and keep his voice from shaking while responding "That's right," Shohei nodded lightly while smiling. Then, as if nothing had happened, he started chatting with Masanobu about champagne.

I wonder if he noticed...that it's the same as Kazuki's ring... He's wearing his...

Wataru's thoughts raced as he looked at Yuichi, but maybe he had already prepared himself regarding the ring, since he didn't seem to be uneasy. Of course, if he'd wanted to hide it from his brother he could have taken it off beforehand so he probably didn't care if it happened. The shadow on his eyes didn't change, and that troubled Wataru's heart.

I wonder what in the world Shohei is thinking.

He was sharp by the look of him, and he didn't seem like the kind of person to toss around meaningless conversation. But it would surely seem unnatural for Wataru to offer what sounded like an excuse when he hadn't exactly been plied with questions. He didn't even know how much Shohei knew in the first place.

"I was thinking a boy like you is a rare type."

At the same time, that could also be applied to Yuichi.

For a boy of the same generation to wear an accessory was quite typical. But, when it was a ring it had a deeper meaning, and the design was a little too simple to dismiss as just mere taste. Not to mention the fact that neither Yuichi nor Wataru had any other precious metal on them, and they weren't the type to deliberately adorn themselves.

When rings were popular back in high school, people just bought them on a whim, not thinking too deeply about it. That they would come to have such special meaning was a development well beyond

Wataru's expectations.

This kind-of seems like it's going to be trouble...

Wataru had a sure feeling this second night was going to be difficult.

He sighed softly, surrounded by the complicated thoughts in Shohei's unreadable eyes.

"...Wataru, Wataru."

They had to walk about five minutes from the restaurant to the hotel. As Wataru strolled along the promenade, using the prettily lit-up facade as a guide, he was suddenly overtaken.

"What is it, Asaka?"

"Yeah...sorry for keeping quiet about Shohei."

"......"

I don't know what to say, since you waited until now to apologize. Shohei had taken it upon himself to cover the dinner bill, and Yuichi was even now in the midst of laying into him for it. Thanks to that, Wataru didn't know who to thank, and was internally at a loss for what to do.

Whether he realized that mental state or not, Masanobu spoke reservedly.

"Actually...I'd like to talk to you for a bit, if you don't mind."

"Uh, but..."

"I know. It won't take very long. And they look like they're right in the middle of things."

As Masanobu indicated, the Kazuki brothers hadn't looked back for a while now. It was a repetition...of Yuichi trying to give his brother the money for dinner, and Shohei vaguely evading it. Wataru slowly stopped walking, and looked up with a face that hid his determination.

"All right. We're going back to the room anyway, so if I hurry afterwards I'll catch up to him soon."

"Is it all right not to say anything to Kazuki?"

"...Right now, he might not even hear it if I do."

"Yeah... Well, why don't we sit on that bench for the moment?"

Urged away, Wataru cast a fleeting glimpse at the retreating Yuichi. If he were to tell him here "I'm going to talk to Asaka," it was as plain as day that his mood would hit rock bottom. However, Wataru wanted to know Masanobu's true feelings. No matter what, he didn't want to think that the same person he'd exchanged a farewell handshake with in the rainy park had come all the way to Okinawa simply out of amusement or a taste for mischief. He had nothing but his own eyes with which to confirm his true intentions.

The promenade was built to encircle the hotel site, just separating the private beach from the building. With Wataru next to Masanobu, surrounded by the sound of waves at night, it somehow became forgettable who he'd come on the trip with. Concealing vague regret, Wataru purposefully stretched his arms high. In actuality, his body had become stiff from the sheer unexpectedness of meeting Shohei.

"Are you okay? You must be confused at tonight's sudden development too, right?"

"To be honest I am. I never even dreamed I

would see you and Yuichi's brother in a place like this, so far from Tokyo."

"It looks like Shohei meant to come here all along."

"Is that so..."

I knew it, he thought in response, and Masanobu let out a small sigh. He slowly crossed his legs, and said while gazing at the dark sea:

"Having said that, it is true that he's here on a business trip. The hotel here is famous, so he got a job from someone to build a villa on a solitary island. You know about his work, right?"

"Just a little... But, he's amazing if he did the plans for a hotel this big."

"Yeah, I respect him too. Maybe he's something of a genius. He gets talked about all over the place from individuals and businesses, even in areas that have nothing to do with his jobs. The house I got Kazuki to help out on will finally re-debut as a gallery by next month, so come by and hang out."

"......"

"Oh, sorry. That's right, you're about to go into exam mode..."

Hearing the apologetic voice, Wataru kept quiet and nodded his head. Masanobu hadn't changed at all, quietly conversing this way. He was delicate, kind, and sometimes sharp enough to be surprising. What kind of man could Shohei Kazuki be, for him to say without hesitation that he respected him?

"Wataru, have you heard of Sette D'oro?"

Masanobu suddenly uttered the unfamiliar name.

"Sette D'oro..."

"I didn't think you had. It's the name of a group that gets talked about quite a bit in the world of architecture. Shohei is one of their founding members. It's an office made up of seven first-class architects, and he's their leader and director. Shibuya live houses, local broadcast halls, suburban development reclamation projects, stuff like that. You've probably seen at least one of their projects."

"But, he's so young..."

"You're right. Shohei is their youngest member. If he didn't have talent, nobody would follow him. In addition, he has the wits to skillfully bring together architects who're very proud. So, like I said., he's something of a genius."

"It's like..."

"Hm?"

"Like...of course he's Kazuki's brother..."

At that point, Wataru ran out of things to say. He'd been constantly overwhelmed since first meeting Shohei, but it made sense considering who he was. Even Yuichi had seemed a regular "little brother" in front of him. The number of words they'd exchanged had been few, but each time Wataru opened his mouth he was scared he'd be seen through to the heart.

"Um...why do you think Shohei came to see Kazuki?"

It took nerve to hear the answer, but Wataru resolutely asked the question.

"When I was asked about the ring, I thought...maybe he knows. That I'm going out with

Kazuki. And so..."

"That's why I came, too."

"Eh..."

"Of course, it's no lie that I'm interested in Okinawa's residential architecture. But the reason I hitched a ride on this business trip was that I knew that Shohei intended to meet up with you two."

"Asaka..."

This time, Wataru was speechless at the unexpected confession. Masanobu had definitely been anticipating what would happen tonight since they saw him at the cafe. In short, it meant he had tricked Yuichi and Wataru by showing up seemingly coincidentally and pretending not to know anything. To Wataru, that was a bigger shock than anything else.

"H-How could you do that? I believed in you...!"

"Wataru..."

"I mean, Kazuki had an obviously nasty look on his face, so I think you were uncomfortable, too... But you know, I was a little happy to get to see you. I thought it was an amazing coincidence that it happened in a place like this, and since it was you we could talk without hiding anything even with Kazuki there. So I..."

"...That's all?"

"Wha?"

After Wataru had gone on and on, Masanobu answered back with this short question. Bewildered by the unexpected words, he shrugged his shoulders in a really disappointed way and repeated, "That's all."

"Huh.   I figured there was some heartfelt emotion behind 'I was a little happy to get to see you.'"

"Wh-What are you talking about?!   What I'm trying to say is...!"

"I know.   Sorry, sorry.   Well, I wasn't really making fun of you.   But you know, the reason I couldn't say anything when I met you two this morning was Kazuki..."

"Kazuki?"

"Because he seemed to be in such a bad mood."

"......"

Wataru had no comeback.   Even if he disliked him in the first place, Yuichi's attitude towards Masanobu's showing up on a trip that was supposed to just be for two had been immature and unlike him.   That Masanobu seemed to calmly let it slide off him didn't really seem to bother him, but it's no surprise that he was ticked off deep-down.

However, Masanobu surmised this from Wataru's expression and he quickly denied it.

"No, no.   I didn't keep quiet on purpose, I couldn't say anything.   I thought, you know, if I'd said then that I was with Shohei, it would have ruined the whole day.   Kazuki has good intuition, so he seemed to notice something was up, but if even you found out his brother was in the same hotel, wouldn't it have made you worry too much to enjoy the trip?"

"Well..."

"So, even though I thought it was selfish I kept quiet.   At any rate, Shohei planned to contact Kazuki, so you'd have found out by tonight anyway...but, I was in the wrong. Sorry."

Being apologized to so seriously, Wataru hastily nodded his head. Simultaneously, he muttered Thank goodness in his heart.

Masanobu was the kind of person Wataru thought he was, after all. He had a kindness different from Yuichi's, the owner of a heart considerate of others' feelings. Wrapped in feelings of relief, Wataru at long last regained his smile.

"I'm sorry, too. I got angrier than I should have..."

"That's understandable. Even I was terribly nervous the first time I met Shohei. Originally, I was introduced to him by someone in the business connected with that house we remodeled, but he has such powerful eyes. Even though all he's doing is smiling and looking at me, it's like he's read deeper into me than I wanted him to. But, thankfully, he seems to have taken a liking to me, and sometimes he has me do part-time work at his office. Looks like being Kazuki's upperclassman scored me high points, too."

Masanobu laughed modestly, but of course his abilities were more than likely appreciated. Even Wataru, who'd known him only a short time, knew that he had superior talents. If that weren't the case, Yuichi would never regard him with such hostility for being so similar to himself.

"Then...you're working together this time, too?"

"No, I'm unrelated to this job of his. But I was told that the hotel tab is free when you travel with him. Two men in one twin is kind of irksome. But, like I said before, he intended to meet up with you two, so I thought it best if I was with him."

"Why is that?"

Wataru genuinely found that mysterious. He could understand why Masanobu was somehow kind to him since he reminded him of where he used to be, but he never thought it would be taken this far.

"Why are you so concerned about us...?"

"Because I'm a hero of justice."

"Eh..."

"As far as you're concerned, that is."

"......"

"Hero of justice" was no doubt a fitting thing for the grinning Masanobu to go by. While turning red Wataru hastily told himself he was being made fun of.

"Hey, Wataru."

"Y...Yes?"

"No joke, Shohei is tough. I don't even know what excuse he used to choose to come to Okinawa, or what he's trying to convey to Kazuki. What I do know is that he casually said 'I want to see Yuichi sometime while he's in Okinawa.' But naturally, the pressure is all on Kazuki this time around. What Shohei says will have bearing on the course of your relationship."

"What Shohei...says?"

"Right. So, I came with him. So you wouldn't be at a loss when the time came that Kazuki was occupied. I could probably be of some use."

"Asaka..."

Those words lightened Wataru's heart a little, as it had been filled with anxiety. Feeling like he could finally relax some, he let out a long sigh. He hadn't planned on relying on Masanobu's good will, but he felt a natural surge of courage just from someone being concerned about them. He stood up vigorously from the bench, holding the ring on his left hand up to the light and gazing at it.

No matter how out the ordinary things got, the weight of one ring didn't change. Yuichi had once said to Wataru "Restricted happiness is better than the freedom of solitude," and his matching ring was surely the symbol of that. However, he had chosen his path on his own, and he wanted no regrets regarding that.

"A tough opponent...eh..."

Maybe once they'd surmounted the obstacle of Shohei, they'd become stronger.

Hoping for the best, Wataru brought his left hand back to his chest.

Yuichi's mood was even fouler than anticipated.

Hurrying back to the room, Wataru was met by a sullen face. It was clear that Yuichi was quite angry. But even so, without sounding categorically condemning, he asked where Wataru had been and what he was doing. As there was no way the observant Yuichi wouldn't have noticed, Wataru had prepared himself and said frankly and honestly, "I was with Asaka."

From there, silence continued for five whole minutes. Yuichi sat on the edge of the bed, a torturous look on his silent face. Unable to find a way to start conversation, Wataru kept quiet and leaned against the wall. He had gained a lot from his conversation with

Masanobu, but he wasn't confident whether Yuichi would honestly listen to that the way he was now.

"So, I'm sorry..."

Unable to endure the silence, Wataru tried apologizing. He knew an apology wasn't what was sought, but there wasn't anything else to say. Yuichi sighed a little, and simply turned his even more darkly clouded eyes wordlessly towards Wataru.

"Kazuki..."

It was the first time he'd been looked at by such piercing eyes, and a pain the sharpness of which he'd never felt before ran through Wataru's heart. They had had small quarrels plenty of times, but those had been nothing more than communication for them to find out more about each other. All that was coming from Yuichi's eyes this time, though, was sad rejection. While feeling at a loss, Wataru was pressed for a way to somehow patch things up.

"Uh, I'm really sorry for disappearing without saying anything. But..."

"Somehow, I had a feeling it would turn out this way."

"Wha...?"

Wataru stared confusedly at Yuichi after the sudden murmur. Yuichi blinked slowly several times, then with eyes just a little closer to normal he opened his mouth again.

"Since this morning, when we saw Asaka. 'I'm with an acquaintance.' seemed like a shaky explanation. So, I thought to myself. It must be some 'acquaintance' whose name would make my mood worse if he mentioned it. There couldn't be anyone like that but my brother."

"......"

"If my brother was with him, it couldn't be any coincidence. Even so, he played his stupid little game."

It was a shock. Even though he'd been sure that Masanobu was all that caused Yuichi's childishly smoldering reaction, on the underside of his cold attitude he'd still paid attention to his partner. In that case, maybe his overt way of dealing with it was so that he could read Masanobu's expression.

"Kazuki...you're really sharp..."

"Anyone would figure it out soon enough. You're pro-Asaka, so you were simply deceived."

"Pro-Asaka...now, come on."

"Aren't you? You had a happy look on your face the instant you saw him."

"Heh?"

At some point the contents of the conversation had inclined towards jealousy. Just as Wataru was amazed because he had been admiring him, he was also deeply relieved that Yuichi was finally back to his old self.

He moved away from the wall bit by bit, shortening the distance to the bed. As no fault-finding look had flown his way, Wataru took another relaxed step towards Yuichi. Yuichi watched the meager effort with a smiling gaze just modest enough not to show he'd noticed it right away. Once time had passed and he arrived in front of him, he wordlessly indicated for him to sit down next to him.

"...The reason you've been odd since this morning was because of your brother."

Wataru spoke slowly while staring at the white wall after sitting next to him on the bed. There was no answer, but he could hear a sigh of what sounded like self-abhorrence.

"I heard various things about him from Asaka. He knew he was taking a business trip to Okinawa to meet us, but not why. So, out of concern, he came along."

"I don't like it. Why does he have to meddle like that?"

"Because he's been worried about us since before. But..."

"Hn?"

"I think you and I are fine on our own. I'm thankful for Asaka's feelings, but this is a problem between you, me, and your brother."

"What if he's opposed?"

In the twinkling of an eye, the question striking at the core of the issue was on the table. Wataru was silent for a moment, then asked back, "Is he opposed?"

"Kazuki, you came back with him first, right? Did he say something?"

"...No. But, no other reason for him to be here comes to mind. I still don't know how he found out about you and me... I think this is probably a purposeful restraint."

"Restraint?"

"Yeah. Just because we're on a trip, it doesn't mean we're free from everything. Maybe that's what he's trying to say. It'd be like him. He'd never come out and honestly say he was opposed. His opposition burns passionately, and I know it. ...Damn it!"

Yuichi hit the bed angrily with his left fist and bit his lip. He had probably rarely experienced situations like this where there was nothing he could do. If the opposition had been open he could plan a counter-attack, but if he didn't move carefully here he was capable of wringing his own neck. Realizing this made his irritation run all the more deeply.

"Kazuki, you didn't take your ring off?"

When Wataru spoke up softly, Yuichi looked at him as if surprised. At the silent nod in his eyes, Wataru once more moved his lips carefully.

"Even though there were many ways you could have deceived him, you didn't. I think that because he grasped how resolved you were, even your brother had to hint at being opposed. Even though we could've smoothed over just the surface, piling up makeshift lies, you didn't demand that of me. I'm very proud of that. The reason you kept so quiet in the restaurant was because you'd have felt bad if I worried too much and couldn't enjoy the food, isn't it?

"Well..."

"That was some good fish. Why don't we eat there one more time before we leave?"

Holding Yuichi's tight fist in both his hands, Wataru tried smiling to cheer him up. Until now, he'd been saved by Yuichi many times. With his pushiness backed by affection and behavior full of self-confidence, he'd always said unwaveringly, "Be in love with me."

However, this time, things were different. From the perspective of Yuichi's personality, even if he said rough things, deep down it should still have been wrenching to cause pain or worry for his family. Even so, with Wataru in front of him he would probably force himself to look fine and say, "Don't worry about anything."

Wataru found that very charming about him. He wanted to help out in this predicament between relatives and boyfriend. For that, he'd have to keep his own presence of mind.

"I'm fine. I'll walk along beside you."

"Wataru..."

"I love you. I love you far more than anyone. I don't think that I can make the whole world understand with these feelings alone. But, don't be worried. I swear I won't waver."

After asserting that with their eyes locked, Wataru extended his arm to Yuichi. The next instant, he was pulled strongly by the wrist and embraced as tightly as possible. His hot palm tantalizingly groped Yuichi's back, and a shivering sigh went sweetly through his neck. His clumsy words must have gotten through, since Yuichi's warmth was filled with more happiness than usual.

"...Smart-aleck."

The remark sounded mixed with a smile and, possibly, tears. Wataru had his eyes closed and was satiated with the sound, as he imagined what expression Yuichi must have worn as he said it.

"You really are getting more and more brazen.

You ain't forgetting you're my servant now, are you?"

"...I remember."

"Then, kiss me."

While offering subtly abusive words, Yuichi softly disengaged himself. Smiling, Wataru brought his lips closer, and just before he would kiss he found himself being kissed. A slight fever was born of the pressing lips, and melted its way to fingertips. Mischievous tongues intertwined, and while conversing in an exchange of sighs, the two held each other for some time.

The lips parted with a sense of reluctance, and the sighs gently drenched the distance between their chests. Next, embraced slowly as if to cherish the lingering memory, Wataru unconsciously let out a small breath.

"Earlier, when you smiled and said 'That was some good fish.'"

"Eh...?"

"It reminded me of the first time I saw your smile."

"Kazuki..."

Wataru's face unknowingly went red at Yuichi's whisper.

That referred to when Wataru lost his favorite ring, and then by-chance Yuichi found it and secretly returned it to Wataru's desk. Because he had no proof-positive it was Wataru's, Yuichi had watched from hiding to see what would happen, and when he saw Wataru's smile he unexpectedly fell in love with him.

"Starting that day, I knew the real me."

"......"

"For the first time in my life, I realized I wanted something I didn't have. I struggled and suffered alone, and because of that I couldn't even speak up to you. While I'd decided I wouldn't do anything futile, I secretly made a ring of the same design as yours. I was shocked myself at what the heck I was doing. Even now when I think back to myself at that time, it's too much for me to handle."

Maybe his memories of the time had reawakened as he talked, as his voice came to sound a bit ashamed. No one would probably ever believe that Yuichi, graced with good looks and superior intelligence, ever worried over unrequited love like some typical high schooler. It felt all the more strange for the one he was in love with to be Wataru, the one now in his arms. Wataru felt like he'd been dreaming ever since he learned that the reason Yuichi concealed his love was that he was afraid of being ridiculed and treated maliciously.

"I finally understood that I loved you, Wataru. What it meant to be in ecstasy. And how selfish and narrow-minded a person I was. Until then, I was coolly composed about everything to the point of it being laughable. Because I could easily and quickly handle anything I had to do, I was leading a flat life soaked in lukewarm water."

"You were gentle and well-behaved, and nice to everyone but me."

"...Right. To everyone but you. You were the only one I could never beat. So I was scared to be around you. I thought I'd keep myself as distant as possible so you wouldn't see through my thoughts."

While saying this, Yuichi put strength into his embracing arms so as not to create any distance. In this way, only his tone of voice continued in a plain, controlled way.

"But, this is the way I like me the most. Out of the nineteen years I've lived, I like the me with you jumping into my arms the best."

"Come on...that's such a small thing..."

"It's no small thing to me at all. When I got you, my world overturned. It's many times harder to be loved by just one person than to be liked by everyone for being an honor student. I had lived all that time without knowing that one simple thing."

"Kazuki..."

It was the same for me, murmured Wataru in his heart. When he thought he was hated by Yuichi, he really couldn't express in words how sad it made him feel. That's how much he'd wanted him. Even before he'd realized it was love, he'd wanted only him.

As they held their embrace, time was all that passed.

Yuichi didn't try to initiate anything else, and Wataru didn't particularly think he wanted him to. Feeling each others' warmth this way was right now more important than anything.

There were still a lot of unresolved problems.

Shohei probably wouldn't stop at just restraint, and thanks to exams their time together from here on would be limited.

Even if that was the case, so that their troubles wouldn't go to waste one by one, Wataru remembered everything, Yuichi's warmth, his heartbeat, his sighs. Etched sweetly in his senses, his love with Yuichi would go on growing.

"I love you, Wataru..."

Yuichi whispered the phrase, fingers naturally intertwining with fingers.

Before Wataru could answer, the rings on each of their left hands glimmered faintly. Yuichi's voice saying "a promise ring" revisited Wataru's eardrum for an instant.

A lonesome timbre quietly pulled Wataru out of sleep.

When he looked dully at the clock, it was just about eight o'clock.

"No way..."

As his consciousness gradually became clear, Wataru was filled with unrest. I'd better make sure, he thought, and taking care not to disturb Yuichi sleeping next to him, he softly got to the floor.

"I mean...you must be joking..."

He headed towards the terrace with feelings full of doubt, and extended his hand to the folding wooden blinds. As he timidly opened them, the scenery that spread out before his eyes put him in a mood of despair.

According to the weather forecast, the four days of their stay were to be blessed with clear weather. The forecaster had said time and again that this being the heart of summer, they would need plenty of sunblock.

"...It's pouring down rain..."

Under a dark sky, raindrops pounded against the window to confirm his fears.

It was like dark clouds were hanging over their own future. What made him leap to that conclusion was probably the fact that he was worried about the presence of Shohei somewhere.

Behind Wataru, who was staring at the rainy sky in a daze, there was the sound of a bed creaking. When he hurriedly looked back, Yuichi was freshly awake, and drowsily sitting up. But he seemed to have already noticed the sound of rain, as gloomy eyes glanced at Wataru.

"You're full of energy, Wataru. You woke up early enough."

"Because our trip ends tomorrow. I feel like we shouldn't waste time...but..."

"......"

"I usually don't dislike rain that much. But it didn't have to rain during our trip... First off, this was supposed to be the end of the rainy season for Okinawa. It's like we're been swindled. It's just too much, you know?"

He tried to speak cheerfully to keep things from getting too gloomy, but no matter what he couldn't deny how heavy his words felt. He sluggishly moved away from the terrace and returned to the bed, put his head in Yuichi's lap, and stopped moving like he'd run out of energy.

"Wataru..."

"Hell. Today was the day we were going to the beach."

"Yeah, yesterday the weather was clear."

"That's not what I'm trying to say! What a bad start to the day..."

Yuichi stroked the moping Wataru's diminutive head to soothe him. Just as Wataru was quarreling over ridiculous thoughts like I wish this had happened the first day we spent the entire time in bed...,the hotel phone suddenly started ringing. Yuichi and Wataru looked at each other dubiously, and both hesitated a short time before trying to answer it. But the phone showed no sign of stopping, mischievously stirring up their anxiety.

They went down to the same cafe as yesterday, and caught sight of Masanobu and Shohei having a friendly chat at a table by the window. The two stood out so much, it wasn't necessary to specifically search for them. Fragments of his conversations with Masanobu and Yuichi came back to him, and before Wataru approached Shohei he recalled the light tension.

"Wataru, are you really sure about this? We should just go somewhere else..."

"Kazuki, you worry too much. It's all right, we've only been invited to eat breakfast together."

"But your smile is frozen in place."

"Ugh..."

Hearing the casual observation, Wataru hurriedly took a deep breath. Whatever Shohei was thinking, if they turned their backs to him now it would be like affirming that they felt guilty about their relationship. He didn't want to spoil their hard-earned trip with feelings like that. Yuichi had reluctantly accepted that argument

of Wataru's, and accepted the breakfast invitation even though he felt disinclined to.

"Good morning."

"Good morning, Fujii. It's too bad about this unfortunate weather today."

Diametrically opposite Masanobu, who returned a quiet smile, Shohei returned the greeting cheerfully and in a carefree manner. From the look of things, he had already finished eating breakfast, and more than half the coffee in his cup was gone.

"I...I'm sorry. Have you been waiting a long time for us?"

"Ahh, not at all. Actually I got a phone call from a client, and I've got to get going."

"Whatever. That's a bit much after waking someone up with a phone call."

"...Yuichi. I didn't really mean you. I'm apologizing to Fujii."

Shohei leisurely brushed off his brother's abusive language, and got up slowly from his seat. Almost as if he'd read Wataru's mind and how he was at a loss for anything to say, his smile asked "What?"

"Because there's no time, we can get better acquainted next time around."

"Uh, um, thank you for paying last night. I heard from Kazuki that you ultimately covered the dinner bill...though I'm a bit late in thanking you..."

"Don't tell me that's the reason for that nasty look?"

"Eh?"

"Yuichi. He's had that sour look ever

since yesterday, and it really does nothing for his attractiveness."

He tried to keep from laughing as he said it, so in any case it didn't seem like he was really angry. Yuichi looked offended, and Shohei whispered even more delightfully "...See?" in Wataru's ear.

"Why don't you take a picture? Other people rarely get to see that face."

"Uh, no, I..."

"Well, even among family I'm about the only one who sees it. Yuichi's a good boy."

"Good boy..."

With the person in question listening, that was a line that unmistakably dropped the surrounding temperature to below zero. Wataru once again hardened a smile on his face, and softly moved away from Shohei before Yuichi's mood worsened.

He's kind of an amusing person, he thought honestly. He exhibited natural talent for his work, enough to make someone like Masanobu say he respected him, yet his scheming dark eyes were somehow innocent. Moreover, they weren't the kind a child would have, but were bordered by a unique color refined by various lights and darks. That certainly could be one aspect that would make you want to read too deeply into things.

However, the rest seemed a little scary. How cunning would one have to be to get a man like Shohei? His wife, who Wataru had met once before, was a beautiful woman with girlish features, but if he had the chance Wataru thought he would very much like to ask about how their romance began.

"Wataru. Let's go get food."

"Huh?"

"Quit spacing out. This place is a buffet. C'mon."

Lightly thumped on the back by Yuichi, Wataru's reverie was unexpectedly shattered. The moment he came back to himself with a start, his eyes once again met with Shohei's, who was looking pleasantly back at him. Wataru was bewildered by just the atmosphere and that look, but beneath the bright illumination the word "handsome" was the best match for the owner of that manly face. He didn't really resemble the slightly fine-lined Yuichi, but Wataru was forced to admire their fraternity when it came to their impulsive but precise behavior.

"Hey, let's go."

Maybe Yuichi was none too impressed that Wataru was dwelling on Shohei, so he brusquely urged him on. As if he'd suddenly thought of it, Shohei murmured "Oh, right." inside his mouth.

"Breakfast didn't work out, but shall we all eat lunch together?"

"I don't think so."

In the blink of an eye, Yuichi spurned the offer.

"We're heading home tomorrow. We don't have time to be hanging out with you."

"That's an extreme thing to say. I'm flying back to Tokyo this afternoon."

"But aren't you here for work? Enough sticking your nose into your brother's privacy, take your assistant there with you and go home."

"Assistant...   Kazuki, I'm just sitting here drinking karela tea..."

Masanobu spoke innocently, as he'd calmly been watching the exchange. Wataru hurriedly tried to scold Yuichi, but the sigh Shohei let out surprised him, and he ended up looking over that way.

"I swear, little brothers are selfish things. Who do you have to thank for staying here at such a low rate...?"

"Wh-What brought that up all of a sudden?"

"Thank goodness for your accomplished, genius brother, right? It's rare of you to ask for a favor, so don't forget that I pitched in and helped here. Or that Masanobu gave you a job to help you raise all your spending money."

"......"

"I thought, what kind of person were you bringing with you to go to all that trouble?"

Shohei's voice was tinged with a tone of banter until the end, but his eyes were serious beyond the point of laughter. Yuichi was silent, looking for the words to say, and Wataru patiently resisted the urge to open his mouth for fear that he'd say something careless.

"...Shohei. Are you all right on time?"

The one who first broke the silence was Masanobu, who had finished his tea. With an air of refinement all his own, he grinned as he compared the three of them and moved forward.

"Aren't we going to take the luggage out together? Then, you'd best go back to the room once."

"Yeah, you're right. You'll feel relieved to sleep

alone tonight, won't you?"

"Yes. I'll take you up on your offer to stay a bit longer."

Shohei nodded at Masanobu's words, and returned the cigarettes on the table to his breast pocket. Yuichi was about to say something, but instead he faltered. Shohei threw a glance his way, but then kept quiet and started to walk. Wataru quickly bowed his head, then shifted his gaze to Yuichi beside him.

"Kazuki... You sure about this...?"

"......"

"Your brother's going to leave like this. Things are all vague, and you don't know when you'll be able to really talk to him next, much less when there'll be a chance for all three of us to talk..."

That's right. Shohei might not be pressing the issue of talking to us because he's going to wait and see what we do before he decides how to handle things. If he's doing this restraint thing and then waiting for a reaction, I'm definitely against letting things end hazily thanks to an evasive attitude.

"Hey, Kazuki..."

Yuichi didn't move. As if conveying a furious internal conflict, only the color of his pupils became more and more stern. He knew Shohei best. Perhaps he couldn't see what it was he was supposed to do to win against him. For Yuichi to be that cautious, a man like Shohei must be a very costly person to have as an enemy.

"Kazuki..."

"Oh. Shohei forgot something. I'd better chase

after him."

"Huh?"

"See, that silver lighter there.   I could have sworn he said it was a present from his wife..."

"Asaka, wait! I'll go!"

Shouted Wataru, and as Masanobu started to reach out he nimbly snatched the lighter out of his hands. The next instant, he shook himself free of Yuichi's voice trying to detain him, and wholeheartedly took off running.

"That was a surprise. Wataru's pretty fast on his feet."

"Wataru..."

Left behind, Yuichi stared in amazement at what had happened so quickly.

Masanobu laughed reservedly, and asked full of playfulness:

"Well then. Oh by the way, what'll you do about breakfast?"

After he rushed out of the cafe, Wataru was easily able to locate Shohei waiting for an elevator at the end of the wide corridor. But, for some reason he hesitated to call out to him.

Because...

It sure is easy to get caught up in all this...

The two elevators were of an art deco design, but it was spread out enough not to make it seem too gaudy, and it brought about a moderately high-class feel. Shohei stood before them with his back straight, his fair figure showing an un-Japanese, pleasant charm.

Kazuki is that way too...wherever he is, he's something more than the atmosphere he's in.

Shohei looked cool in his suit the night before, but the coolness of this morning's ensemble of a navy cotton jacket and nice pants matched up well with the atmosphere of this unreal resort hotel. As Wataru admired him for his obvious involvement in planning the place, the elevator arrived with a light ching sound.

"Ah, wait! Shohei, please wait up!"

He rushed over to him with small running steps, and quickly held out the lighter in his hand. But Shohei didn't seem especially surprised, and instead said "Thank you." as he accepted the forgotten item with a smile.

"You didn't need to be in such a rush, though. I had no intention of getting on in the first place."

"Huh?"

"Because I had a feeling you'd be here."

Looking back at Wataru with a roguish look, Shohei spoke these unexpected words.

Yuichi sat violently upright in a seat, with a look on his face that said This ain't no time for breakfast. But, he might have seemed sulky if he'd not said anything, so he looked languidly at Masanobu and said:

"...Why did you pull that?"

"Pull what?"

"Him leaving his lighter behind practically on purpose. You and my brother make quite a team."

"A team. If that's a compliment, I'm very much honored."

With no obvious intention of answering the

question, Masanobu dexterously poured more tea into his cup.

"How about some karela tea, Kazuki? They say it's good for your health. When the girls in my circle heard I was going to Okinawa, they all at the same time asked for some. They're bitter to eat, but the tea is slightly sweet..."

"I really don't care about tea. More importantly, you know, don't you? Why my brother suddenly came to Okinawa. Where the hell did he hear about me and Wataru...?"

After getting that much out, Yuichi shut his mouth in surprise. Masanobu's smile, not fragmented or trembling, showed signs of being artificial. When he thought about it, ever since he'd first met him on the college campus he'd strongly sensed some kind of pretext.

This guy's the same as me.

Walking another, different life. Another version of himself.

In that case... thought Yuichi as a feeling of unrest once again reflected sharply in his eyes.

"Could it have been...you...?"

Masanobu said nothing, slowly tilting his cup.

"Uh...so, that was on purpose after all..."

Wataru was just a little surprised that he'd used the words "after all" unconsciously. But when he thought about it rationally, he got the feeling it was impossible that Shohei would carelessly forget something that had been a present from his wife. Yuichi probably tried to stop him because he realized this.

"Shohei, you thought it was me who would come instead of Kazuki?"

"Well, you know. He doesn't fall for this kind of thing. But, the fact that he didn't come with you shows he has quite a bit of faith in you."

"What do you mean?"

"He probably thinks you won't make any blunders, even alone with me."

Confronted with steadily more confusing lines, Wataru fell silent for a time. This was because he very much didn't feel he could match words with an adult the likes of Shohei. However, maybe Shohei hadn't just said that to be nice, as he had a satisfied-looking smile on his face.

"It's true that I have work to do, so we'll have to stand around here and talk..."

"Ah, sure."

"You're...Yuichi's lover, aren't you?"

"...That's correct."

As there was no point in hiding it now, Wataru steeled himself and nodded firmly. Until now, several people including his sister and best friend had found out, but this was the first time he'd had to confirm it for someone in this way.

"You're honest."

Shohei seemed caught off guard for a second by such a direct answer. But, clashing with his serious expression, his eyes softened suddenly and he began speaking lightly.

"Actually, when I got a call from Yuichi that he was going to Okinawa, I thought for sure he'd found a girlfriend. As you can see, isn't this hotel excellent for couples and families? Thanks to the abundance of female-oriented facilities and services, it's good for groups of girls, too. But, it's a waste of money for men to stay here together. For picking up girls is one thing, but this isn't a hotel for two men to stay at while sightseeing."

"......"

"Thinking I might have been narrow-minded, Masanobu and I tried staying in a twin together this time. Sure enough, my pet theory wasn't mistaken. Well, he and I share interests, and he's good looking so it didn't hurt a bit to be together with him. It's just...sleeping in the same room as him. In some ways it interfered with the concept of the drama I created here."

It wasn't a problem of money, Shohei went on to say. And he said that no matter how close to free the hotel bill was, if your roommate was a male friend it would result in most guys feeling twice as empty.

"But, Yuichi says he doesn't mind. That must be because it'll make you happy, Fujii. Since you're going into exam preparation mode after the summer, he wants to let you have your last breather. I said, in that case I'll have two singles prepared, but he turned that down with a laugh."

"So...you thought that was strange?"

"Well, that's not all. But, Yuichi is quite a stubborn person, so it really is rare for him to ask for a favor from my connections. I think, maybe it's the first time ever. He was always the type to do things himself, and unlike me, he's never been troubling to our parents."

Wataru was reminded of the phrase "good boy" from earlier, and it made him want to sigh. From his point of view as an outsider, Shohei was quite used to doing things at his own pace. He carried his adult composure now more than ever, but there was probably a time when he couldn't control his intense nature. Being raised after a brother like that, there was no way kind Yuichi could be said to be disobedient. Being compared to Yuichi was probably hard on him, too.

The elevator which had been passed up once had let off riders and returned once again. Shohei glanced down at his watch, and shrugged as if to say he'd reached his time limit.

"...This marks about a year, doesn't it?"

"Wha?"

"Your relationship. I confess, it's been about that long ago since Yuichi started wearing that sullen face of his. I imagine you see more of his faces than I do. Enough so that pictures are unnecessary."

"Shohei..."

The elevator door opened, and Shohei got into the empty car. He stood in the center and faced Wataru, and while pushing the "open" button said something unexpected.

"I was going to say this if you'd followed me without hesitation."

"Eh..."

"Tell Yuichi this. That I...will become his enemy."

Shohei spoke his harsh declaration cheerfully,

like he was talking to an old friend.

Before Wataru could answer, Shohei's finger left the "open" button and the doors shut quietly.

I'll stay here until Wataru comes back, he had thought, but it had already been fifteen minutes. Yuichi naturally remembered his hunger, and looked from the table with food on it to outside the rain-covered window. The rain still showed no sign of stopping, and both the ocean and the pool looked like the opposite side of hazy curtains of water.

"It's all right. They said in the weather forecast it would clear up by afternoon."

He must have finished his meal with Shohei, because Masanobu was as carefree as always. From the start he hadn't expected Yuichi to answer, and he kept talking on his own.

"But still, Wataru's taking a bit long. Maybe he wasn't able to see Shohei. Or maybe he got lost on his way back... This hotel is terribly big after all."

"...I heard the plans took a year to do."

"A year, eh? It was the first hotel handled by Sette D'oro. They beat out the most influential contending office in competition, an unprecedented selection that became the talk of the industry."

"My brother was totally happy at the time."

His gaze fastened on the outside the whole time, Yuichi muttered like he was talking to himself. Be that as it may, Masanobu consented deeply, and Yuichi giggled on one side of his face.

"That's not accurate. Competition is when you

compete with a rival. He's the type that, when there's an opponent he must defeat, he becomes unexpectedly lively and starts to demonstrate his true ability. That's how it was when he met my sister-in-law. She was a sheltered young woman with a congressional secretary for a fiancé, and he snatched her away in an instant."

"Is...that so?"

"If he gets serious, nothing will go not according to his say. I've seen it play out many times since I was a kid. But he's not eccentric enough to move for no reason other than me being in a homosexual relationship. So, he wasn't overly concerned about the situation with Wataru."

Effectively, this meant that something made him take time out of his busy schedule to come to Okinawa. I was naive, Yuichi regretted bitterly but it was too late. If Shohei wasn't done with just this restraint, how would Yuichi protect Wataru in the future? That was all that had been on his mind for a while now.

"Kazuki."

As he was irritatedly staring at the rain, a voice tinged with restraint spoke up. Yuichi came back to reality all at once, and quickly turned to look at Wataru standing beside him.

"Sorry I took so long. I got a little caught up talking to Shohei."

"Wataru..."

"I kind-of feel relieved, and now I'm crazy hungry. It's still breakfast time, isn't it? Since you waited for me, let's go get something."

"W-Wait a minute. What's this about feeling

relieved?"

Yuichi had only been imagining dark things, so hearing this unexpected word from Wataru had him taken aback. What could it mean for him to "feel relieved" after talking one-on-one with Shohei? Maybe he'd unexpectedly taken a liking to Wataru, and said that he was on their side. In that case, he didn't need to worry about unknown obstacles any further. There was nothing more reassuring than Shohei supporting them, if he was.

Yuichi looked at Wataru again in anticipation. If he heard the answer he was expecting from those lips, they'd go down to the beach right now, rain or shine. Just as his chest swelled with that hope, some rather unexpected words flew out of Wataru's mouth.

"He said he'd become your enemy."

"Eh...?"

"He told me to tell you that. It wasn't a restraint, he came out and said it."

"You're...kid...ding..."

"I was surprised myself. Shohei just said that and left for work, so I had no choice but to come back."

"No way..."

Yuichi wasn't the only one left speechless by Wataru's report. Masanobu, who'd also been listening, had a look of disbelief carved on his features. Subjected to the piercing gaze of the silent pair, Wataru uncomfortably pouted his lips.

"Well whatever, let's just get some food. Aren't you hungry, Kazuki?"

"How..."

"Huh?"

"How can you be so calm? If he's become my enemy, that means he's opposed..."

"Yeah. It means he's opposed. It's all right, I understand that too. But strangely enough, when I found out his stance clearly, instead I felt relieved. I mean, now I don't have to have it bugging me. You said that yourself, didn't you, Kazuki?"

It definitely wasn't just bravado; Wataru seemed to feel this way from the bottom of his heart. Sure, they had discussed last night that the restraint alone had their hands tied, but Yuichi wasn't able to change his mindset that easily. That being said, what in the world was this decisiveness of Wataru's?

"Do you realize how bad it is for him to be against us?"

Once he came back to himself, Yuichi flared up.

"It's not just a maybe. He's going to completely interfere with us!"

"I realize that. I'm not exactly fine with it, and I figure we need to talk about it. But, I'm really not that scared."

"Not scared...Wataru, he's talking about Shohei."

This time, Masanobu spoke up amazedly. This was because his position was different than Yuichi's, but he still knew Shohei well. To him, a normal high school student like Wataru should not have been saying he wasn't scared of this.

"In any event, that's just..."

"But it's the truth. You know, don't you, Asaka? That just about the only feeling I've had for Kazuki is love. Because of that I was always irritated by and hateful of myself, and it couldn't be helped that I was worried about being hated by him... But, now this time it's different."

"Wataru..."

"The only thing I fear for is Kazuki's heart, so as long as I'm sure of that I'm not scared of anyone else. I've thought that all over again. Even if our opponent is Shohei."

"......"

"Besides, Shohei seemed a bit excited. I think he's probably looking forward to what will come of us. That's a different feeling than hatred or abhorrence, isn't it? Right, Kazuki?"

Faced with a look full of trust, Yuichi's doubt dissolved bit by bit. He hadn't completely gotten his bearings back, but even so he barely managed to nod "Yeah."

Shohei had probably touched on this part of Wataru.

There was no direct doubt in his eyes, and no matter how dangerous things seemed he essentially never swayed. The light was hidden in an outside appearance too ordinary to show it, but that made the moment of light leave all the more of an impression. Maybe when Wataru exchanged a glance with Yuichi and ran off with the lighter with hardly a word, he could sense an urge to get an answer out of Shohei.

Then, Shohei might have been led by the

impulse to see what expression Wataru would have when he learned that Shohei intended to stand as an obstacle.

Being his brother, Yuichi understood that feeling well.

He had once acted coldly towards Wataru on purpose, and it resulted in him loving him all the more.

"Wow... Wataru never ceases to amaze."

Masanobu's small utterance filtered through the distance between the three.

Just as Wataru smiled awkwardly, his stomach made a loud sound.

Masanobu had said it would stop by afternoon, but unfortunately the sky was still heavy and dark. Wataru and Yuichi had finished breakfast and gone back to the room, and for now they decided to reschedule their day's agenda.

"We should at least have bathing suits ready. There're beaches all over the place, and we can just go if it clears up. That aside, is there anywhere with a roof you want to go, Wataru?"

"Hmmm...I'd say the market. I saw it in the guidebook, but aren't there lots of different stores inside? We can buy souvenirs there, and at noon go to that cafeteria you mentioned..."

"You just got done with breakfast and you're talking about lunch?"

Hearing the voice filled with heartfelt admiration, Wataru got sullen and turned red. Because they'd eaten until the last minute, the time was already past ten. He certainly wouldn't be able to easily digest everything in his packed stomach in two hours. Maybe as a reaction to the stressful exchange with Shohei, he'd gone back for heaping platefuls so many times it amazed Masanobu and Yuichi.

"Oh yeah, I wonder if Asaka has already gone out."

"Beats me. He was saying he's going out to look at some 400-year-old houses."

It was actually a careless answer that practically said "Who cares about Masanobu?" Wataru smiled ruefully and wondered what in the world they had talked about after he took off in pursuit of Shohei.

Masanobu had said earlier that Shohei's flight was the earliest one in the afternoon. Yuichi wasn't unaware of what his intention was bringing that up in the middle of the meal. However, he said nothing, and Wataru didn't mean to do anything unnecessary. He already had his own answer within him, and Yuichi's emotions seemed to have calmed down considerably. In that case, there was no problem until after they returned to Tokyo, so for now it was best to enjoy the trip as much as possible.

"We talked about so much, and it really ate up a lot of time."

They stuffed what they'd need for the beach into a bag, and Wataru left the room behind in high spirits. Yuichi followed behind him quietly. The reason he behaved a little more slowly than usual was probably because he had a lot on his mind and he sometimes became preoccupied. But the cloud that had descended on his eyes since last night was completely gone, so there didn't seem to be much to worry about. All they had left to do was pass the final night of their trip in enjoyment.

"Huh?"

Wataru cheerfully got off the elevator, noticed that the atmosphere in the lobby was different than usual, and tilted his head. The terrace seats were closed off by a glass door because of the rain, but despite that there was a crowd gathered around.

"What's this? I hear them talking, but..."

"Sh. Take a close look, Wataru."

"Eh?"

"It's a wedding. They're using the lobby as an impromptu chapel, and having a public wedding."

In the direction Yuichi indicated, there was a deep crimson aisle stretching out. The gathered spectators, while being careful not to step on the cloth, watched the couple attentively from a distance as the couple listened to the priest's sermon.

The ocean, subdued from the rain, spread out beyond the glass behind the priest, and just like a stage set, an elegant pillar with a gold cross set into it had been built. A large number of wooden chairs had been lined up on either side of it, and people who might have been relatives were sitting in them. The white mermaid-design wedding dress looked very good on the slender bride, and here and there complimentary voices were heard.

"What a surprise. You can have a wedding even in a place like this..."

"Of course you can. At any rate, my brother was the first one."

"Eh!"

"Because he wanted to hold his wedding while looking at the ocean, he maneuvered here and there and presented an option like this to the hotel. They accepted, and it seems it's pretty tough to reserve it now."

"So that's how... Shohei's really..."

An image of Shohei in great joy over having his wedding the way he imagined it, and securing a job along the way floated before Wataru's eyes. It was so pleasant, and the instant Wataru was about to break into a smile, Yuichi abruptly grasped his left hand.

The ring on his ring finger enclosed in Yuichi's palm, Wataru was a bit surprised. The people around them were absorbed in the wedding so it didn't stand out, but Yuichi's hand was very reassuring, and seemed to be appealing to something.

"What..."

"To be honest, I was going to say this after you got done with exams."

"......"

"Starting next spring, would you like to live together?"

Wataru's heart pounded hard once. If the prelude to a hymn hadn't started then, it might have resounded through the lobby. He stared at Yuichi's profile in silence, and quietly digested his words.

Starting next spring, would you like to live together?

To Wataru at that moment, that was the best idea

he could ever think of. But at the same time, since he was a minor there were clearly a number of problems, and it would be a tough dream to fulfill.

"Uh, Kazuki..."

"We're going to go to different colleges, and I think our circumstances and relationships are going to change in various ways. But if we come home to the same place every day, I have a feeling another world will come into being there. I want to make both of those important. Just a few hours a day is fine, so I want a place we can both have."

"Yeah..."

"...Well, to put it simply, all I want is to have more time together with you."

Yuichi turned his head and looked at Wataru with smiling eyes. Wataru gently returned the smile, and gently, meaningfully, nodded.

The more I hear "I'll be with you more," the more I'd rather it was "I'll be with you forever." We can't have a "marriage" like the couple in front of us, but instead of promising eternity to each other at the start, we can arrive at eternity at the end.

Even if it's an illusion, and doesn't exist anywhere.

Wataru was always having these feelings.

It was like an eternal moment that would not fade.

"A place together..."

Wataru was immersed in his happy imagination for a while, and a determination-concealing Yuichi once again spoke up.

"...By the way. Sorry, but could you come with me to the airport from here?"

"Wha?"

"We might not make it in time, but I want you to come with me."

"So...you're going to see Shohei. Is that what that means?"

He asked as if to confirm, and Yuichi answered "Yeah" with unusually tense eyes. It made his resolution seem all the deeper, and the sound of his voice was heart-piercing.

"I thought I told you last night. I can't win against you. In this world, it's annoying, but there's another person I can't beat. That's...my brother."

The way Yuichi spoke, he seemed reluctant from the bottom of his heart. No matter how grave he looked on the surface, he was actually quite a determined person, so that vexation probably wasn't half-baked.

"So, today I'm putting an end to that. I've decided. I will come out above him. If I don't, I know he'll interfere with my living with you. And, I can't let him do that."

"Kazuki..."

"So, now I'm going to the airport to declare war. I've had enough of being arbitrarily messing with."

Yuichi turned briskly while holding Wataru's hand. If they didn't hurry, they wouldn't have much time before the flight. But as he was about to call out to the valet waiting at the entrance, he caught sight of Masanobu waving from inside an unexpectedly prepared car and his eyes went wide.

"Asaka..."

"That's no good, Kazuki. On a rainy day like today, how could you be irresponsible enough to leave an elder behind and run off to the airport...and with your prized lover in-tow, to boot?"

"Why're you here...didn't you already leave...?"

"...So you didn't notice me after all. I was watching the wedding too. So maybe that set it off, but there was this couple all happy about something, and I happened to hear a thing or two. Hey, who cares, just get in. I'll be your special chauffeur just this once."

Urging the pair standing in mute amazement, Masanobu signaled for them to hurry and get in. Wataru hurriedly followed after Yuichi into the back seat, feeling both thankful and timid as he opened his mouth.

"Uh...thanks, Asaka. But, why are you going this far...?"

"Come on, Wataru. Didn't I tell you my true identity?"

"Huh?"

The slightly peevish sound was mixed with a taste of banter.

"I'm a hero of justice as far as you're concerned."

Masanobu looked over his shoulder and smiled as he gazed fondly at the bewildered Wataru.

"Shohei! Wait a minute, please, Shohei!"

Wataru raised his voice as loud as he could at the back of the head even now heading towards the departure gate.

"Shohei!"

"...Just when I wondered who was making so much noise."

Shohei finally stopped walking and turned around with a smile on his face.

"Are you all right, Fujii? Your face is bright red."

"Well...uh, but...it sure is a good thing you're tall..."

"Yeah, I stand out anywhere. I never thought you'd come to see me off, though."

"...That's not really why I'm here."

As Wataru looked downward and caught his breath, from behind him Yuichi appeared, hardly out of breath at all. For an instant, Shohei wore a dubious expression, but he soon hid it underneath the smile.

In the now tense atmosphere, the brothers wordlessly faced each other for a short time. But the final boarding announcement for Shohei's plane began, so naturally he couldn't keep it up.

"Sorry, but that's the time limit."

Shohei picked up his small travel bag from the floor, and grinned at the two.

"Yuichi, I know why you've come. You heard my message through Fujii, didn't you? I've clearly given my stance, so you think on it. We'll continue this in Tokyo."

"...Bro. Do you by some chance find things to have gotten interesting?"

Maybe he hit the mark, as Shohei kept smiling and didn't answer.

Not caring, Yuichi looked him in the eye and said defiantly:

"Actually, I think so too. It makes me excited. I came this far to say that."

"Excited? You?"

"Yeah. Not just me; Wataru feels the same way. It'll be that much more gratifying when we make you approve of us. Chances like this don't come around too often. Do they?"

"......"

Shohei seemed to be unusually overpowered by the fearless look in Yuichi's eyes. Neither Yuichi nor Wataru failed to notice that he showed his first dim shade of unrest.

"It really has gotten interesting."

Before long the edges of his lips raised tightly, and Shohei spoke in a serious voice. The cold depth of it was more serious than anything Wataru had heard from him to date.

"Fine, try making me approve. I look forward to what you two will do."

"...You got it."

Yuichi nodded slightly, and opened his mouth again.

"But, there's one thing I want to ask you. How did you know about me and Wataru? I doubt it, but does Asaka have anything to do with it?"

"Masanobu? Yeah, now that you mention it he seems to know a lot, too."

"I knew it..."

"Whoa, whoa, that doesn't mean he said

anything. Of course, he might have helped me put the pieces together. I meant to lure the truth out of him, and when I mentioned in front of him that I might be going to Okinawa, he asked right away if he could come with."

"Bro...you even tricked Asaka...?"

Yuichi was too taken aback to say anything else, and Shohei just smiled unashamedly at him.

"Over and above that, you're forgetting one important person."

"Important person?"

Yuichi had no idea, and he knit his brow hard. In the first place, there was no one besides Wataru next to him who was truly important. Shohei saw his brother this way, shook his head as if he wanted to say it was sad, and sighed exaggeratedly.

"This is a good chance, so I'll warn you here. Don't flirt recklessly in front of a child. Kid or not, Takako is a splendid woman."

"Takako?!"

"What a bad uncle you are. You turned down her proposal, and if that wasn't enough you kissed someone else in front of her. Now she's convinced that you'll marry Fujii. She said her dream future is one where the three of you live happily in the same house."

"......"

"She's drawing pictures every day, in her room. Pictures of her, your, and Fujii's dream house."

It was so much information that Yuichi had nothing to say at first. He didn't think Shohei would possibly believe what his five-year-old daughter said. Of course there had to have been more of a foundation for this conclusion, and it was still easier to grasp that Masanobu had leaked the information.

"But, that was so Takako would give up on me..."

"Even at five a woman can tell the difference between a joke-kiss and a real one."

That must be why she backed down so easily, he could have said, but no answer was spoken.

"Well, even without that, I always thought it was weird. I don't know if our parents noticed, but over the past year you've become strangely unsociable. Proportionally, you've probably become more handsome, too. And you've definitely brought your ring that matches Fujii's with you the whole way, haven't you?"

"Matching ring...you mean, you knew about that this whole time...?"

"Yeah. I heard that from Takako, too. Don't underestimate the eyes of children. When you two came to visit her, she noticed you had the same rings. Kirie said so, too."

"Ah...my sister-in-law did..."

Takako wasn't as childish as they had thought. Put another way, it probably meant that was how much she liked Yuichi and Wataru.

"As her parent, I feel pity for Takako. It was amusing, so I thought I'd leave you be for a while, but I was a bit interested in seeing what level of feelings you two had for each other. In Tokyo, though, there isn't much in the way of chances to observe you, is there? So there you have it."

"So...your answer to all this is 'enemy.'"

"You have to face serious people seriously. That's my policy."

"......"

Hearing Shohei's explanation, Wataru shot a look at Yuichi saying, "Like I said, stop doing that in front of children." This being the case, the one who'd created the biggest obstacle in their history was Yuichi himself.

"I..."

"Stop right there. Sorry, but I really don't have time."

Interrupting Yuichi as he was about to say something, Shohei stared fearlessly back at the two of them.

"Enjoy today as much as you can. You're back in Tokyo tomorrow, aren't you?"

"Bro..."

"They say people become fools when they're in love..."

Just before he started walking, Shohei spoke one last time, with the face of a big brother:

"But you've become much more of a man."

"This is the first time I've ever seen rain fall on the sea."

Wataru let slip his soliloquy, and Yuichi abruptly softened his expression.

"What, Kazuki? Did I say something funny?"

"No... It's that you've said 'This is the first time I've seen' a lot on this trip."

"I guess I have... Well, this is my first encounter with Okinawa itself. It's all good, I'm enjoying it."

Wearing the hood of his nylon parka over his head to ward off the rain, Wataru leisurely walked down to the beach. He could sense that Yuichi followed behind him. Due to the sense of security at his back, Wataru kept walking without intentionally turning around. The waves broke onto his sand-covered sneakers, and sent countless little shell fragments tumbling as they returned to the sea.

The intensity of the rain had abated considerably, but there still wasn't anyone crazy enough to come down to the sandy beach. In Wataru's hazy field of vision, the rows of orderly arranged white deck chairs looked like a movie set.

"Even so, what are we doing here?"

Wataru asked Yuichi this with a pleading tone while narrowing his eyes and gazing at the horizon. Yuichi seemed to laugh faintly, but it was small enough to be lost to the sound of the rain.

Once they saw Shohei off and returned to the parking lot, Masanobu had already left. Wataru had taken off running upon arrival at the airport and didn't know, but it seemed Masanobu had entrusted Yuichi with the car keys and nonchalantly said "You can borrow this." Yuichi had complained that he didn't like that remark, but as this allowed Wataru and he to be alone the rest of the time, he might not have been thankful but at least he probably had no reason to be resentful.

"But, why'd we drive to the ocean? Didn't you say 'if it clears up'?"

"I changed my mind. In the first place, monopolizing a deserted beach is not an easy trick to pull off."

"Don't tell me that's the only reason?"

"There are some things you can't do on a sunny day, you know."

As Yuichi spoke with a smile, he seemed to be loved even by the rain. The moment he headed for the wet sandy beach without carrying an umbrella, the sensation of the raindrops became gentle like silk.

"But, that Asaka, I really can't let my guard down with him. When I expressed distrust to him, if it was a misunderstanding then he should've just said so. But instead he just frigging smiled ambiguously."

"When you think of that, maybe Asaka found this amusing after all."

"Well...who can say...?"

The vague answer of Yuichi's politely said to cease the line of inquiry. The phrase "As far as Wataru's concerned" meant that even Wataru was strangely conscious of it. Up until now Masanobu was somehow concerned about things, but he had never taken invasive actions in-line with today's events. It felt like something inside even him had definitely changed over the course of this trip.

However, Wataru gave up thinking about Masanobu any further than that. What was important to him now was sharing this time with Yuichi. His eyes were filled with him, and he wanted to devote his whole heart.

As he was leaving Shohei said "You've become

much more of a man," and Wataru truly did think that. Yuichi declared "I will come out above him," and his eyes had said that that future was a certainty. That exemplified the basis of the conceit that was Yuichi Kazuki. So, it was a sure thing that he would pull it off.

"...It sure is peaceful."

Yuichi murmured solemnly and abruptly. Wataru silently nodded, and felt his rain-chilled hand clasped. A bit farther apart than usual, they stood stock still, firmly holding hands as if they had made vows in the lobby. Yuichi asked in a reserved tone, "Aren't you cold?"

"Shall we go back to the hotel and take a hot bath or something? The spa there seems nice and spacious."

"Before that, let's head back to the market and eat some blue fish. There're still places I want to go. The weather forecast was off, but I intend to enjoy myself with everything I've got until tonight."

"You're telling me to come with you? What an outrageous servant."

"Yeah, but...it's our last night."

At the slightly lonely murmur, Yuichi bopped Wataru on the head with his free hand. Mixed with the sound of the rain, he said meaningfully, as if to himself "There's the option of not sleeping all night."

"All night...whoa."

"What? Aren't you supposed to do whatever I say until tomorrow? Then keep quiet and don't complain. I won't let you disagree with my requests."

"Th-That...depends on their nature!"

"What're you turning red for?"

Faced with a malicious look and a smile, Wataru was firmly at a loss for words. But, even if it was an utterance that normally could be written off as a joke, precisely because what happened the first day happened, he couldn't be off his guard. Then, there had been a sense that they had all the time in the world, but in a few hours it would be evening. They still hadn't gone in the water, and they hadn't even seen Shuri Castle or even the yanbarukuinas.

"I'll bring you here again anytime."

As he grew more and more opposed to what Yuichi was saying, Wataru answered back sullenly.

"Can you afford to be so carefree? Shohei's serious. Next time we might not be able to just up and go on a trip. I can hardly imagine what he might do..."

"I'm serious too."

Yuichi was still smiling, but he answered in a voice filled with confidence. The rain was tapering off, and all the visual lines were even more clearly defined that before.

"I'm serious. Therefore, I will not lose. What I said to my brother at the airport was true. I'm so excited it's weird. Like the time when I got you."

"Kazuki..."

"Because you're here, it doesn't feel like I'll lose. And in the first place, I'm not soft enough to let anyone besides you win. My brother...I knew I'd have to face him like this someday."

He suddenly let go of the hand he was holding, and nimbly embraced Wataru's shoulders. Hot body warmth passed through the damp clothes, and Wataru unconsciously heaved a sigh. As if that was a signal, Yuichi's left hand slowly removed the hood of the parka. A glance upward caught the wet ring shining.

"Even if it's not simple enough to put into words,"

Just before their lips met, Wataru's were moistened with a whisper.

"If we're together, I think everything will be fine…and fun."

Their wet cheeks rubbed against each other, and the rain-mingled kiss served in place of a promise.

You said it, thought Wataru with his throbbing heart.

Yuichi knew how to have fun in any situation. So, there was nothing to worry about. Wataru would continue to grow bit by bit from here, and believe in him.

As they embraced, Wataru was immersed in the resonance, and the voice over his shoulder suddenly became cheerful.

"So, that takes care of vows once more. Shall we head back to the market?"

"Heh?"

"What? Weren't you the one who said he wanted to eat? The blue fish."

"Uh, but...I mean, before you said something about the spa..."

Looking at Wataru's bewildered face, Yuichi suddenly leaned over and met his gaze. Caught by the determined eyes, Wataru gave up and let out a sigh of surrender.

"Okay, okay. I'm a servant, right? As my master says, I will go anywhere with him."

"Now that's dedication. Then, we'll go back to the hotel after all?"

"Hey come on, enough's...ah, well..."

"Hm?"

"Well...either one works for me..."

When he reluctantly let out his true opinion, he found himself surrounded by a burst of laughter. At some point the rain had stopped, and far off the sky was gradually starting to regain its radiance.

"We might as well...get going."

Before Wataru could ask where, Yuichi started walking off with the car key tucked in his palm. The people here and there who had come down to the beach followed him with their eyes, as if fascinated.

Oh man, again?

Wataru muttered to himself the same thought as their first day there. I guess there's no helping having to worry about lots of extra things when you have a boyfriend who stands out. Even when it's just us, there're always unrefined glances from every direction.

But, I have to admit it's also true that I'm proud when I think he's my boyfriend.

"Wataru, what're you doing? Hurry it up."

Indifferent about the attention from everyone, Yuichi turned around and called back.

"You've got guts, making me wait."

"I hear you... I'm on my way."

Surrounded by the sound of waves after the rain, Wataru smiled as he took a step into the future.

Afterword

Hello, this is Kannagi. It has been a long time, but I hope you all have been well.

About a whole two years after "Ring Finger," here is the sequel in print. All you readers are probably surprised, but the most surprised is in the end myself, the author. However, every time I got a message from my home page and whatnot saying someone was waiting for it to come out in paperback, my joy more than my bewilderment is what grew bigger and bigger. For that reason, I'm happy to after a long time get my fill of the "Ring Finger" world.

I wrote that it's been about two years, and naturally lots of things have happened during that time. I suppose the biggest thing was the comic adaptation by my illustrator Hotaru Odagiri. When talk came up about it being serialized in a magazine, I made a absurdly excited sound like "Hyoeee!" Every time I turned the page of the magazines they sent, I let loose an emotional sigh "Uohh!" of uncertain meaning. The comics collected in this way and that produced a lot of new readers. I think that there are probably many people among those reading this afterword who "got into it from the comic." I tried hard to make this novel enjoyable for those people too, so how did I do? To be honest I was a little nervous, but I wrote while looking forward to my own reunion with those guys. I think it would be nice if

I was able to convey those feelings.

So. As you read, this book saw some unexpected developments. Out of all of it, the introduction of Yuichi's brother was probably the highlight. The character of Yuichi is admired as being "too good to be true," so what kind of man would his older brother be...and he was already an adult with a wife and child to boot. I was worried, thinking about this and that, and the result was going beyond that kind of "noble" character and giving birth to what should be called a "kingly" character. Of course, I poured my personal tastes 100% into him, so it goes without saying who my favorite became this time. I can't drop any spoilers in the afterword, but the natural effect of his appearance is great changes to the love between Yuichi and Wataru. The new character Asaka, too, is cunning in how he will be involved with the two from here on.

However, up to this point there have been quite a few instigations, but it feels like the more I write the stronger the relationship between Yuichi and Wataru gets. They say lines the author never even foresaw, and they love in a way that makes me want to tell them to do this themselves. By my nature I write a lot of sweet stories, but even in the Kannagi world there are no lovers who are a match for these two. Even that occurred to me at some point. This is probably influenced by all the words from readers in support of their love. And, the power of Miss Odagiri's lovely stirring illustrations must be quite effective too.

Okinawa becomes the stage for the lovey-dovey story. I love that place too, to the extent that I periodically cry out "I want to go to Okinawa!", and at the time I was writing this story I was working double time, yet I went there to collect data. I took pictures and shot video everywhere, brought home all my materials, and bought three guidebooks in all...but, my head was so filled with thoughts like "This is where Yuichi and Wataru..." and "If they went on a date there, where would they eat?" that I didn't get a single tape or picture with me in it. Even so, I'm thankful I went because I was able to condense my short time there (two nights, three days) tightly into thinking about the novel. If anyone reading this hasn't ever been to Okinawa, by all means please go. I took my Okinawa-connoisseur little sister (to the point that she once planned to live there) with me in place of a driver, and she unexpectedly ran into her ex-boyfriend she'd broken up with years ago while eating breakfast in the hotel cafe (which appears in the novel). Well, her big sister had the sense to say "Oh, well, I'll go buy a souvenir over there..." and ran off. I guess, sweet coincidences like that just happen in Okinawa...

I had nothing but fun researching other various things while writing this book. Regarding the "Renovation Research Society" Asaka belongs to, this time I bought books about architecture here and there, and thanks to that I was able to discover new personal enjoyment. Yes, I have always loved looking at floor plans and the like. My parents are tatami mat dealers, so I had fun as a child going to see new houses being built with my father. Renovation is different from that, but you see TV programs about giving new life to old buildings all the time these days. I can't get enough of things like that dealing with houses. It might be a bit of a problem if it grows into my getting into ruins, though... (But I do like ruins.)

And so, here we have a big commercial! At the start of this I touched on the comic adaptation, but actually in October a "Ring Finger" drama CD is going to go on sale! This means you get to hear Yuichi and Wataru talking with your own ears. I plan to communicate the details in the magazine Chara or on my home page, but in any case please check it out. You may wonder about the cast, but it's the awesome golden combination of Takahiro Sakurai as Yuichi and Kenichi Suzumura as Wataru. I'm going to be eagerly anticipating this too.

This became the last topic, but my illustrator Hotaru Odagiri has come along with me together expanding the world of "Ring Finger." I thank her for the always beautiful Yuichi and adorable Wataru. It's rather a shame that I can only thank her once a month, but this sequel might not have taken shape without her cooperation. That's how much her many beautiful illustrations gave me courage and determination while I was writing the book. Thank you very much in that way as well. Also, thank you to Mr. Yamada my editor for his sharp opinions. Every time we finished one of our customary midnight business calls, I would feel strangely high. I know I can be a bother, but I'm thinking I want to keep applying myself, so here's to a good ongoing business relationship.

And, and, more than anything all of you, my readers. Thank you for waiting these two years! If you wish, I would love to hear your thoughts and such. Tell them to me from your heart. The rough summer heat is still lingering, so please watch out for your health. Until next time...

Humbly yours,
Satoru Kannagi

Profile

Satoru Kannagi
Writer
Born 3/26
Aries
Blood Type A
From Ibaraki Prefecture • Residing in Tokyo

Writing a book about Okinawa made me very much want to do an extended stay there. But, if I was in a land with that kind of climate I'd probably go to the beach every day and get nothing done. I guess a one-bedroom apartment in Tokyo suits me best...

Hotaru Odagiri
Illustrator

Born 10/5
Libra
Blood Type O
Residing in Tokyo

Manga artist, works include "Time Lag," "Only the Ring Finger Knows" (Tokuma Shoten), and others...

WHO AM I?

COLD SLEEP
a novel

by Narise Konohara

Having lost his memory in an accident, Toru Takahisa tries to reclaim his past. Fujishima is the man that takes Toru in, claiming to be his friend. Find out what happens in this exciting new novel.

ISBN# 1-56970-887-8 $8.95

june
junemanga.com